SEASONAL APPETITE

SEASONAL APPETITE

A Chef's Celebration of
Vermont's Seasons

MARCIE KAUFMAN

iUniverse, Inc.
New York Bloomington

Seasonal Appetite
A Chef's Celebration of Vermont's seasons

iUniverse books may be ordered through booksellers or by contacting:

iUniverse
1663 Liberty Drive
Bloomington, IN 47403
www.iuniverse.com
1-800-Authors (1-800-288-4677)

Because of the dynamic nature of the Internet, any Web addresses or links contained in this book may have changed since publication and may no longer be valid.

The views expressed in this work are solely those of the author and do not necessarily reflect the views of the publisher, and the publisher hereby disclaims any responsibility for them.

Creative direction and artwork copyright by Jeff Gold

ISBN: 978-0-595-43121-2 (sc)
ISBN: 978-0-595-87464-4 (ebook)

Printed in the United States of America

This book is dedicated to the memory
of my father, George Kaufman,
and to my mother, Sylvia Kaufman,
for their cherished love and support.

Contents

The Spring Menu 2

The Summer Menu 4

The Autumn Menu 6

The Winter Menu 8

Introduction 11

The Spring Season 12
- Appetizers 14
- Breads 25
- Soups 33
- Salads 40
- Entrées 46
- Desserts 61

The Summer Season 74
- Appetizers 76
- Breads 86
- Soups 93
- Salads 100
- Entrées 109
- Desserts 119

The Autumn Season 134
- Appetizers 136
- Breads 146
- Soups 156
- Salads 166
- Entrées 174
- Desserts 184

The Winter Season 196
- Appetizers 198
- Breads 210
- Soups 218
- Salads 226
- Entrées 233
- Desserts 245

Source Directory 255

Index 269

Preface

Appetite is an innate wisdom to satiate the sensation of hunger and thirst. Foods adaptive to climatic change of season ensure nourishment, regulate body temperature, and sustain life. Bear witness to the symbiotic connection between animal and plant life thriving in any given season. SEASONAL APPETITE celebrates this wisdom.

Spring, summer, autumn, and winter menus outline the four chapters of the cookbook. Each menu displays an enticing collection of seasonal appetizers, breads, soups, salads, entrées, and desserts designed to satiate and nourish appetite. Recipes pair with seasonally available foods, grown and produced in Vermont. Peruse a season's exceptional menu selections. Savor the recipes. What whets the appetite?

Recipes for preparation use the U.S. measurement system of weight and volume, and the Metric measurement system of units for successful results. Classic dishes from the body of my professional work have been selected to harmonize with the taste, texture and appearance of Vermont's seasonal ingredients.

Satiate seasonal appetite with a meal prepared to celebrate the bountiful fresh flavor of Vermont's spectacular seasons.

I would like to acknowledge the many talented chefs and cooks I've had the privilege of working with in my professional career. This book could not have been created without you.

Thank You.

SEASONAL APPETITE

The Spring Menu

Appetizers

Salmon Galantine ~crème fraîche

Poached Blue Mussels Vin Blanc

Fusilli with Pancetta, Button Mushrooms, and Baby Spinach

Baby Artichoke Tart

Bread Assortment

Petit Pains

Stone Ground Whole Wheat Loaves

Focaccia

Poppy Seed Dinner Rolls

Soups

Red Pepper Cream

Cream of Carrot-Ginger Soup

Chicken Consommé

Borscht

Salads

Baby Beet, Arugula, and Hazelnut Salad ~hazelnut vinaigrette

Spinach and Feta Cheese Salad ~calamata olive dressing

Asparagus, Vermont Blue, and Mâche ~blue cheese vinaigrette

Spring Greens ~maple-balsamic vinaigrette

Entrées

Dressed Brook Trout stuffed with Bell Pepper Pesto
~red wine sauce, steamed spinach and shallots

Lamb Chop and Fava Bean Ragoût
~whipped potatoes

Poached Turbot with Tomato-Herb Broth

Chicken Roulade of Prosciutto, Asparagus, and Havarti
~morel cream sauce, fiddleheads, and russet potato

Desserts

Pistachio Sponge Cake with Mascarpone Cheese Frosting
~chocolate sauce

Strawberry Charlotte Russe ~strawberry sauce

White Chocolate and Maple Mousse in Almond Tuile

Key Lime Tartlets ~fruit salsa

The Summer Menu

Appetizers

Crab-Stuffed Chive Crêpe Pillows ~roasted corn cream

Spinach Lasagna

Apricot-Glazed Shrimp Cocktail

Penne with Shallot, Garlic, Roma Tomato, and Basil

Bread Assortment

Pain Ordinare

Miniature Corn Muffins

Black Currant Dinner Rolls

Cracked Wheat Rolls

Soups

Corn Chowder

Sorrel Vichyssoise

Gazpacho

Fresh Tomato-Basil Cream

Salads
Watercress Salad with Avocado and Shaved Asiago
~creamy garlic dressing
Ratatouille Salad with Fresh Buffalo Mozzarella
Caesar Salad
Chopped Salad with Spicy Chicken ~bacon ranch dressing

Entrées
Roast Pork Loin with Rhubarb Sauce ~glazed yellow and green beans
Tequilla-Lime Swordfish with Roasted Corn and Poblano Salsa
~parsley red potatoes
Teriyaki-Marinated Tri-Tip Sirloin
~parmesan and gruyère whipped potatoes
Fillet of Sole with Fines Herbs à la Meunière
~tarragon carrots

Desserts
Ganache Chocolate Mousse Cake ~chantilly cream
Fresh Plum Tartlets ~black pepper-scented ice cream
Raspberry and Grand Marnier Soufflé Glacé ~fresh raspberry sauce
White Chocolate Timbales ~bing cherry sauce

The Autumn Menu

Appetizers

Caramelized Sea Scallops ~clementine-fennel relish

Fettuccine Alfredo

Gateau Escargot ~red wine gastrique

Tourtière ~apricot-tomato jam

Bread Assortment

Vermont Cheddar Rolls

Rosemary-Raisin Baguettes

Crusty Boules

Triple-Seeded Braid

Soups

Mushroom Cream Soup

Cream of Parsnip

Roasted Acorn Squash and Apple Bisque
~crème fraîche

Billi Bi Soup

Salads

Spinach Salad with Honeyed Spiked Pecans and Gorgonzola
~cranberry vinaigrette

Buffalo Mozzarella, Wild Mushroom, and Vine-Ripened Tomato Salad

Salad of Smoked Turkey and Pecan Rice
~orange-balsamic vinaigrette

Red Bartlett Pear and Fontina Cheese Salad

Entrées

Coq au Vin

Crispy Magret of Duckling with Fresh Cranberry Compote
~creamy wild rice

Wiener Schnitzel ~potato pancakes and red cabbage

Venison Loin Roast with Sun-Dried Cherry Sauce
~sweet potato hash

Desserts

Crème Caramel

White Chocolate Cheesecake ~pomegranate sauce

Tarte Tatin ~vanilla bean ice cream

Hubbard Squash and Crystallized Ginger Tart
~myers's rum chantilly cream

The Winter Menu

Appetizers

Spinach Timbales ~roasted red pepper sauce

Pork Rillettes with Sweet Onion Marmalade and Cornichons

Farfalle with Cremini, Smoked Salmon, and Green Peppercorn

Pan-Roasted Quail with Cinnamon and French Lentils

Bread Assortment

Brown Bread

Parmesan Breadsticks

Pain au Lait

Olive Loaves

Soups

Oyster Chowder

French Onion Soup

Potato-Leek Cream with Crispy Leeks

Cream of Cauliflower Soup

Salads

Bosc Pear with Vermont Blue and Bitter Greens
~balsamic vinaigrette

Citrus Salad

Salad of Escarole, Endive, and Garlic Croutons
~warm red wine-mustard vinaigrette

White Bean and Chorizo Salad

Entrées

Osso Bucco

Bouchée of Lobster, Shrimp, and Broccoli Nantua

Rabbit Blanquette ~straw and hay tagliatelle

Roast Tenderloin of Beef with Sauce au Poivre
~potato dauphenoise

Desserts

Crème Brûlée

Caramelized Almond and Pear Cheesecake

Lemon Tartlets

Mocha Crèmes ~chantilly cream

Introduction

Nestled in the beautiful foothills of Jay Peak, Vermont the chef is home. The solitude of my own kitchen replaces the restaurant's animated discourse. Outside my window is a pastoral landscape of pristine forested mountains, winding dirt roads, verdant meadows, and azure slivers of stream. Nature's breathtaking beauty inspires the creation of this cookbook.

Spring, struggling with cold temperatures, strong winds, and icy rains is nature's new beginning. Our blood thins, our appetites decrease, and our vitality awakens. The birth of nourishing green vegetables whet the appetite for salads of tender lettuces, and the fresh-caught flavor of fish from ice-free rivers, lakes, and streams.

Summer, lush, green, and moist is nature's growing season. The sunlight nourishes our being as well as the gardens'. We refresh the appetite and cool our bodies of summer's heat with chilled vegetable soups, zestful salads, and the juicy sweet fruits of summer.

Autumn is the season of harvest. Forests are briefly painted red, yellow, orange, purple, and gold. Slowly, everything in nature turns within. Leaves dry and fall, and the sap of plant life returns to its roots. We are drawn indoors to the comforting warmth of the wood stove. As our blood thickens in anticipation of winter, the appetite is tempted by the hearty full flavor of enriched soups, and succulent wild game.

Winter arrives confidently with a blanket of white for reflection and recreation. Cold days and long darkened nights persuade the appetite to warm our bodies with velvety-sauced entrées, hot buttery breads, and rich creamy desserts.

Celebrate nature's abundance. Whet, refresh, tempt, and persuade seasonal appetite with inspired meals created in your own kitchen. Listen. Vermont's seasons beckon, *Come home*.

Sincerely,
Marcie

The Spring Season

With the onset of spring, a turf war ensues. Winter is a formidable opponent hurling strong wind, icy rain, and snow upon the land. Eventually, spring reigns triumphant, and the annual renewal of life begins.

The spring garden heralds the arrival of mustard greens, arugula, mâche, cress, baby spinach and lettuces, the tender leaves of dandelion, radish, and beet, and California's artichoke. Shallots, ramps, chives, scallions, and garlic sprouts offer aromatic flavor. Fiddleheads, morels, fava beans, asparagus, radishes, parsnips, broccoli rabe, baby beets, and new potatoes bring fresh flavor to the spring table. Vermont's rivers, lakes, and streams abound with wild trout and salmon. Artisanal cheeses and grass-fed and finished lamb are ready for market. With the pink stalks of rhubarb and the perfume of strawberries, a pie is surely in the making.

Spring is "sugarin' time." With warmer daytime temperatures, and freezing nights, the time-honored tradition of boiling the collected sap of maple trees begins. Pure Vermont maple syrup is the result.

Entice the appetite with a dinner to honor this rite of spring.

Asparagus, Vermont Blue, and Mâche

~blue cheese vinaigrette

Spring's first vegetable, bitter and mildly pungent, mingles with the spicy, piquant flavor of blue cheese, and the mild, nutty flavor and firm-textured bite of mâche.

Poached Turbot with Tomato-Herb Broth

The delicate, fresh flavor of this snowy white, moist, and finely textured fish delivered daily from the cold waters of the North Atlantic, serves the perfect foil to the sweet and sour flavor of Roma tomatoes, the fragrance of slowly cooked onions and garlic, and the anise taste of tarragon.

White Chocolate and Maple Mousse in Almond Tuile

This marriage of rich and creamy Belgium white chocolate with sweet, pure Vermont maple syrup is entwined in a light, airy mousse, and nestled in a crisp confection.

Heavenly.

൭

Salmon Galantine
~crème fraîche

Crème Fraîche

1 cup heavy cream

1 tablespoon buttermilk, fresh and well-shaken

Salmon Galantine

5 1/2 ounces very fresh wild salmon, raw, thinly sliced, very cold

1 tablespoon smoked salmon, very cold

1 tablespoon lightly beaten egg white, cold

4 ounces and 1/2 tablespoon heavy cream, cold and divided

1 tablespoon water

unsalted butter, as needed

3/4 cup cucumber, peeled, seeded, *brunoise* and divided

1/2 cup red onion, minced and divided

salt and white pepper, as needed

24 slices cocktail pumpernickel bread, toasted

1/2 ounce capers, rinsed and drained

dill sprigs, to garnish

Procedure for Crème Fraîche:

Combine heavy cream and buttermilk by stirring in a clean glass jar with a lid. Place in a warm space in the kitchen, lidded and undisturbed, for thirty-six hours.

Refrigerate crème fraîche. It will continue to thicken and will remain fresh for one week. Lightly whisk to serve.

Procedure for Salmon Galantine:

Fill an 11 x 15 x 3-inch roasting pan three-fourths full with cold water. Place pan over two burners, and bring to barely a simmer over a medium flame.

Place food processor work bowl and metal blade into refrigerator until blade is well-chilled.

Half fill a medium-sized bowl with ice and water, and set a smaller bowl on top of the ice bath. Combine raw and smoked salmon in smaller bowl.

Prepare the *mousseline*. Set up food processor bowl and blade. Work very quickly to keep ingredients cold. Process salmon until puréed; scrape bowl and beater, add egg white, and pulse on and off to incorporate. With machine running, steadily add 4 ounces heavy cream in a thin stream; process just until ingredients are blended. Mixture should be smooth but not rubbery, and hold its shape when scooped with a spoon. If too stiff, add additional cream 1 tablespoon at a time until corrected. Scrape mixture through a sieve into the smaller bowl set atop of ice bath, and refrigerate.

Add 1 tablespoon water and 1/2 tablespoon butter into a small saucepan, and bring to the boil. Stir in 1/4 cup cucumber and 1 tablespoon red onion, and cook until water is evaporated. Remove from heat, stir in 1/2 tablespoon heavy cream, and season to taste. Refrigerate vegetables until cold; fold into *mousseline*. Lightly salt the barely simmering water. Poach a *quenelle* of the mixture, taste and make seasoning adjustments as needed. Keep mixture refrigerated.

Lightly butter a 15-inch rectangle of foil. Spread mixture evenly down the center of foil; roll into a tight cylinder, and twist ends to seal. Place galantine on a rack, and lower into water. Poach to an internal temperature of 150° approximately one hour. Remove rack and galantine. Cool to room temperature. Unwrap galantine, and rewrap with plastic wrap forming a tight cylinder. Refrigerate overnight.

Plating:

Arrange three slices of toasted pumpernickel on a small plate to form petals. Unwrap galantine; slice three thin rounds using a hot, dry slicing knife, and place onto toasts. Mound with crème fraîche, and sprinkle with cucumber, red onion, and capers. Garnish with small dill sprig.

Yield:

eight servings

brunoise: to cut to 1/8-inch square

mousseline: a very light stuffing of white meat or seafood with cream and eggs

quenelle: a light, poached dumpling formed into an oval shape using two spoons

Poached Blue Mussels Vin Blanc

Blue Mussel Fumet

dash salt

2 1/4 pounds blue wild mussels

1 ounce unsalted butter

1/2 cup ramps, well-rinsed and finely chopped

1 clove garlic, minced

freshly ground black pepper, as needed

6 ounces dry white wine

6 ounces cold water

dash cayenne

1 bay leaf

Sauce Vin Blanc

8 ounces dry white wine

blue mussel *fumet* (see Procedure)

8 ounces heavy cream

3 large egg yolks, room temperature

chives, minced, to garnish

Procedure for Blue Mussel Fumet:

Scrub mussels under cold running water to remove dirt and beards, and place into a large bowl filled with cold water and a dash of salt. Allow mussels to soak for one hour to release sand. Drain mussels through a colander, and rinse; discard opened mussels. Refrigerate mussels.

Place a medium-sized *rondeau* over a low flame, add butter and melt. Add ramps and garlic, and season lightly with black pepper; *sweat* vegetables. Add wine, water, cayenne, bay leaf, and mussels; cover and bring to the boil. Cook mussels briefly until opened. Transfer mussels into a small bowl with a slotted spoon; discard unopened mussels. Remove mussels from shells; divide equally into four 7 x 1 1/2-inch gratin dishes, and place on a baking sheet. Pour *fumet* through a sieve double lined with cheesecloth into a small bowl.

Procedure for Sauce Vin Blanc:

Pour wine into a small saucepan, and bring to the boil over a medium-high flame. Reduce volume by half; pour into a small stainless bowl, and reserve. Pour fumet into saucepan, bring to the boil over a medium-high flame, and reduce volume to 2 ounces. Whisk in heavy cream; bring to the boil, reduce flame to medium, and cook until quite thickened.

Preheat radiant oven to 450°. Half fill a two quart saucepan with water. Place over a low flame, and bring to a simmer. Set bowl of wine over pan, and whisk until warm. Pour in yolks, and whisk constantly for one to two minutes until thickened. Remove bowl from heat, and whisk in reduced cream mixture. Pour sauce evenly over mussels. *Gratiné* briefly until lightly golden.

Plating:

Set gratin dishes on large plates. Sprinkle with chives, and serve.

Yield:

four servings

fumet: a highly flavored broth of aromatic ingredients and wine

rondeau: a shallow, wide, straight-sided pot with two loop handles

sweat: to cook without color in a small amount of fat over a low flame

gratiné: to brown in a hot oven or under the broiler

Fusilli with Pancetta, Button Mushrooms, and Baby Spinach

6 ounces dried fusilli pasta

olive oil, as needed

salt, as needed

2 ounces pancetta, *medium dice*

6 ounces button mushrooms, cleaned and quartered

freshly ground black pepper, as needed

2 shallots, minced

2 cloves garlic, minced

12 ounces heavy cream

Parmigiano Reggiano, finely grated, as needed

6 ounces baby spinach

Procedure:

Three-fourths fill a six quart pasta pot with cold water; bring to the boil, and salt the water to taste the salt. Cook pasta al dente.

While water is heating, place a small *rondeau* over a medium flame, film lightly with oil, add pancetta and cook until crisp. Transfer pancetta to a paper towel-lined plate, and reserve. Adjust flame to medium-high, add additional oil as needed. Add mushrooms, season with pepper, and cook until lightly golden brown. Stir in shallots and garlic. Whisk in cream, and cook until slightly thickened whisking frequently. Remove from heat; whisk in 2 tablespoons Parmigiano Reggiano until thoroughly combined. Add spinach, and cover *rondeau*. Let stand for one minute, and remove cover.

Drain cooked pasta thoroughly; do not rinse. Add pasta and pancetta to cream mixture; toss well to combine.

Plating:

Spoon pasta into warmed small bowls placed on large plates. Garnish with Parmigiano Reggiano.

Yield:

four servings

medium dice: to cut to 1/3-inch square

rondeau: a shallow, wide, straight-sided pot with two loop handles

Baby Artichoke Tart

1 recipe **Pâte Brisée** rolled 9 x 13 x 1/8-inch, and refrigerated

(recipe follows **Baby Artichoke Tart**)

unsalted butter, as needed

6 baby artichokes

olive oil, as needed

1 tablespoon fresh lemon juice

6 ounces button mushroom caps, cleaned and quartered

freshly ground black pepper, as needed

2 cloves garlic, minced

2 shallots, minced

1/4 cup scallions, white part only, thinly sliced

3 tablespoons parsley, finely chopped and divided

1 Roma tomato, seeded, and *small dice*

4 large eggs, lightly beaten

3 ounces Vermont Chèvre, crumbled, room temperature

4 tablespoons Parmigiano Reggiano, finely grated

8 ounces Gruyère, grated and divided

1 egg combined with 1 tablespoon cold water for egg wash

Procedure:

Preheat radiant oven to 375°.

Remove dough from refrigerator, and allow to soften slightly.

Butter an 8 x 12-inch tart pan. Form dough into pan, and reinforce sides. Place on a baking sheet, and refrigerate. Wrap left-over dough in a sheet of plastic, flatten, and freeze for another use.

Cut off the stems and all tough outer leaves of artichokes. Round the bottoms, and slice into quarters. Generously film a ten inch stainless sauté pan with oil, and place over a low-medium flame. Add artichokes, and cook until tender approximately twenty minutes stirring frequently. Add lemon juice, and cook until evaporated. Transfer artichokes into a small bowl. Adjust flame to medium. Add additional oil to pan as needed; stir in mushrooms, season with black pepper, and *sauté* until golden brown tossing frequently. Reduce flame to low, add garlic, shallots, and scallions, and cook briefly. Cool mixture to room temperature. Stir into bowl of artichokes with 1 tablespoon parsley, and tomato.

Combine eggs in a small bowl. Stir in Chèvre, Parmigiano Reggiano, and 6 ounces Gruyère.

Prick bottom and sides of dough with a fork. Sprinkle remaining 2 ounces Gruyère over bottom of dough, scatter with artichoke mixture, and cover with mixture of eggs and cheese. Brush the sides of tart with egg wash.

Bake until puffed and lightly golden brown approximately thirty-five minutes.

Cool tart on a rack for ten minutes, and remove rim. Slice tart into squares.

Plating:

Place tart slice, centered, on warm small plate. Lightly scatter parsley to garnish.

Yield:

eight servings

small dice: to cut to 1/4-inch square

sauté: to cook quickly in a small amount of fat

Pâte Brisée

2 cups unbleached all purpose flour

1/4 teaspoon salt

3 ounces salted butter, very cold

3 ounces unsalted butter, very cold

1/3 cup ice cold water

Procedure:

With metal blade inserted into food processor, add flour and salt to work bowl, and process briefly to combine.

Medium dice butter, and scatter over flour mixture. Pulse on and off until mixture resembles very coarse cornmeal. Do *not* over process.

Remove lid, and sprinkle dough with water. Pulse on and off until dough begins to leave sides of work bowl. Do *not* allow dough to form a ball.

Pour dough onto a large sheet of plastic wrap, and gently gather. Flatten to a disc, wrap with plastic, and place inside of a plastic bag. Refrigerate dough for three hours.

Yield:

one, large tart shell or six tartlet shells

medium dice: to cut to 1/3-inch square

ॐ
Petit Pains

12 ounces water, 105°

1/2 ounce (scant) dry active yeast

dash granulated sugar

1 1/4 pound bread flour

3/4 tablespoon salt

olive oil, as needed

cornmeal, as needed

unbleached all purpose flour, as needed

Procedure:

Measure 12 ounces water into a warm 5-quart KitchenAid® mixer bowl, sprinkle in yeast and sugar, and whisk to combine. Allow yeast to *proof* for ten minutes.

Attach dough hook to mixer. Add bread flour, and begin *kneading* on Stir speed until dough begins to form. Add salt. Add additional flour or water as needed to achieve a slightly moist dough. *Knead* on speed 2 for six minutes.

Turn dough out onto work surface; *knead* with moistened hands until dough feels smooth and elastic.

Lightly oil a medium-sized bowl. Place dough into bowl, oiled side up, and cover with plastic wrap and a tea towel. Allow dough to rise in a warm area until doubled in bulk.

Turn dough out onto work surface, and lightly flatten; cover with a dampened tea towel, and rest five minutes.

Roll to *3 fold* dough. Cover with dampened tea towel, and rest five minutes.

Scale dough into three, eleven ounce portions. Flatten portions, and place smooth side down on work surface. Cover with dampened tea towel.

Line a baking sheet with parchment, and dust with cornmeal.

With moistened hands, fold sides of portions into center, and seal forming circles. Flip portions over and *round. Place equally spaced on prepared baking sheet, and cover with dampened tea towel. Rise until doubled in bulk.

Preheat radiant oven to 425°. Fill a cake pan with water.

When loaves are fully risen, dust tops lightly with all purpose flour. Place cake pan of water on lowest oven rack.

Slash a cross hatch design into tops of loaves, and place baking sheet on center oven rack.

Hit the cake pan to cause water to splash. Close oven door.

Bake loaves fifteen minutes, turn baking sheet, and continue to bake for ten to fifteen minutes or until deeply golden brown, and bottoms sound hollow when tapped. Turn off oven, and slightly open door. Let loaves remain in oven for five minutes to develop crust.

Cool completely on a rack.

Yield:

three, ten ounce breads

*proof: to allow yeast to rise

*knead: to develop gluten in dough to expand and hold carbon dioxide

*3 fold: Square flattened dough. Beginning at top of the dough, fold one-third down; gently seal seam. Repeat the fold. For the third fold, bring bottom of dough up and over forming a log shape; gently seal seam.

*round: to shape dough into a tight, smooth ball

Stone Ground Whole Wheat Loaves

6 ounces water, 110°

1/4 ounce dry active yeast

dash granulated sugar

2/3 cup plain yogurt

unsalted butter, cold, as needed

3 ounces molasses

7 cups stone ground whole wheat flour, approximately, divided

2 1/4 teaspoons salt

11 ounces water, 115°

safflower oil, as needed

Procedure:

Pour 6 ounces 110° water into a warm bowl; sprinkle with yeast and sugar, and whisk to combine. Allow yeast to *proof* for ten minutes.

Combine yogurt, 1 ounce cubed butter, and molasses in a small bowl.

Pour 2 1/4 cups flour into a KitchenAid® 5-quart mixer bowl. Make a well in the center, and add yeast mixture. Stir mixture to a shaggy mass using a rubber spatula.

Stir 11 ounces 115° water into yogurt mixture. Add yogurt mixture to flour mixture in four parts stirring until smooth.

Attach dough hook to mixer, and begin *kneading* on speed 2. Gradually add 4 1/4 cups flour allowing flour to be absorbed with each addition. Add salt. Scrape bowl and beater. Continue *kneading* and adding additional flour until dough leaves sides of bowl and climbs hook. Knead for seven minutes. Dough will feel a bit drier.

Turn dough out onto a lightly floured board, and finish *kneading* by hand until dough feels smooth and elastic. The dough will lose wetness yet will still be sticky.

Lightly oil a medium-sized bowl. Place dough into bowl, oiled side up. Cover bowl with plastic wrap and a tea towel. Allow dough to rise in a warm area until doubled in bulk.

Gently press fist into dough to deflate, re-cover, and let rise again until nearly doubled.

Turn dough out onto a lightly floured surface, and flatten. Cover with a dampened tea towel, and rest five minutes.

Roll to *3 fold* dough. Cover with dampened tea towel, and rest five minutes.

Butter two 8 x 4-inch loaf pans. Scale dough into two equal portions. Without stretching, flatten to an 8-inch length rectangle using a bench scraper to straighten edges.

Fold top of dough down 1/2-inch, and seal. Evenly fold sides into center of dough, and seal. Roll dough down from top into a log shape, and seal final seam. Repeat procedure with remaining portion.

Place loaves into prepared pans, and cover with dampened tea towel. Allow loaves to rise until completely doubled in bulk.

Preheat radiant oven to 350°.

Slash loaves three times diagonally. Place pans on a baking sheet, and bake for thirty minutes. Turn baking sheet in oven, lower temperature to 325°, and continue to bake approximately twenty minutes or until deeply golden brown.

Immediately turn loaves out of pans onto a rack. Cool completely.

Yield:

two loaves

proof: to allow yeast to rise

knead: to develop gluten in dough to expand and hold carbon dioxide

3 fold: Square flattened dough. Beginning at top of the dough, fold one-third down; gently seal seam. Repeat the fold. For the third fold, bring bottom of dough up and over forming a log shape; gently seal seam.

Focaccia

16 ounces water, 105°

1/2 ounce dry active yeast

1/2 ounce granulated sugar

5 ounces olive oil, divided, and additional for oiling

2 pounds unbleached all purpose flour

7 sprigs rosemary leaves, minced and divided

1/2 cup scallions, thinly sliced

2 3/4 teaspoons salt, divided

1 medium red onion, *small dice*

1/2 tablespoon freshly ground black pepper

Procedure:

Pour 16 ounces water into a warm 5-quart KitchenAid® mixer bowl; sprinkle with yeast and sugar, and whisk to combine. Allow yeast to *proof* for ten minutes. Steadily stir 4 ounces oil into yeast mixture.

Attach dough hook to mixer, turn to speed Stir, and steadily add all of flour. Add 2 tablespoons rosemary and scallions. As dough begins to form, add 2 1/4 teaspoons salt. Add additional flour or water as needed to achieve a moist dough. *Knead* on speed 2 for five minutes.

Turn dough out onto work surface, and *knead with moistened hands until dough feels smooth and elastic.

Lightly oil a large bowl. Place dough into bowl, oiled side up. Cover bowl with plastic wrap and a tea towel. Allow dough to rise in a warm area until doubled in bulk.

Generously oil two, 9 x 2-inch round cake pans, and place on a baking sheet.

Turn dough out onto work surface, and flatten. Cover with a dampened tea towel, and rest five minutes.

With moistened hands, roll to *3 fold dough. Cover dough with dampened tea towel and rest five minutes.

Scale dough into two equal portions; place smooth side down on work surface, and flatten. With moistened hands, fold sides of portions into center, and seal forming circles. Flip portions over and *round. Place into prepared pans, and cover with dampened tea towel. Allow loaves to rise until doubled in bulk.

Preheat radiant oven to 350°.

Combine red onion, black pepper, remaining rosemary, 1/2 teaspoon salt, and 1 ounce olive oil. Spread mixture evenly onto loaves, and spray with water. Slash the center of loaves.

Bake for twenty-five minutes, turn baking sheet, and continue to bake approximately twenty-five minutes or until deeply golden brown.

Immediately turn breads out of pans onto a rack. Cool completely.

Yield:

two breads

*small dice: to cut to 1/4-inch square

*proof: to allow yeast to rise

*knead: to develop gluten in dough to expand and hold carbon dioxide

*3 fold: Square flattened dough. Beginning at top of the dough, fold one-third down; gently seal seam. Repeat the fold. For the third fold, bring bottom of dough up and over forming a log shape; gently seal seam.

*round: to shape dough into a tight, smooth ball

Poppy Seed Dinner Rolls

14 ounces warm water, 105°

1/2 ounce dry active yeast

1/2 ounce granulated sugar

11 ounces high-gluten flour

13 ounces bread flour

1/2 ounce malt powder

3/4 tablespoon salt

2 tablespoons poppy seeds, and additional for dusting

safflower oil, as needed

1 egg combined with 1 tablespoon cold water for egg wash

Procedure:

Measure 14 ounces water into a warm 5-quart KitchenAid® mixer bowl; whisk in yeast and sugar until dissolved. Allow yeast to *proof* for ten minutes.

Attach dough hook to mixer. Add flours and malt, and begin *kneading* on speed Stir. When dough begins to form, add salt. Add additional flour or water as needed to produce a slightly moist soft dough. *Knead* on speed 2 for five minutes. Add 2 tablespoons poppy seeds, and continue to *knead* for two minutes.

Turn dough out onto work surface, and with moistened hands finish *kneading* until dough feels smooth and elastic.

Lightly oil a medium-sized bowl. Place dough into bowl, oiled side up. Cover bowl with plastic wrap and a tea towel. Allow dough to rise in a warm area until doubled in bulk.

Line a baking sheet with parchment.

Turn dough out onto work surface, and lightly flatten. Cover with a dampened tea towel, and rest for five minutes.

Roll to *2 fold* dough. Cover with dampened tea towel, and rest for five minutes.

Scale dough into three ounce portions, *round*, and place on prepared baking sheet. Cover with dampened tea towel, and rise until doubled in bulk.

Preheat radiant oven to 400°.

Brush rolls with egg wash from bottom up to top. Slash each roll once, and dust lightly with poppy seeds.

Bake for twelve minutes, turn baking sheet, and continue to bake approximately eight minutes or until deeply golden brown.

Cool completely on a rack.

Yield:

thirteen rolls

proof: to allow yeast to rise

knead: to develop gluten in dough to expand and hold carbon dioxide

2 fold: Square flattened dough. Beginning at top of the dough, fold one-half down; gently seal seam. Bring bottom of dough up and over forming a log shape, and gently seal seam.

round: to shape dough into a tight, smooth ball

❧

Red Pepper Cream

6 red bell peppers

2 small jalapeño

olive oil, as needed

1 teaspoon fennel seed

1 1/2 cup Spanish onion, *small dice*

1/4 teaspoon dried thyme leaves

1/2 teaspoon garlic, minced

freshly ground black pepper, as needed

1 bay leaf

40 ounces **Chicken Stock** (recipe follows **Red Pepper Cream**)

2 ounces tomato sauce

16 ounces heavy cream

salt, to taste

parsley, finely chopped, to garnish

Procedure:

Preheat radiant oven to 400°.

Place red bell and jalapeño peppers into a small roasting pan, and rub lightly with oil. Roast peppers until skin is lightly charred, turning occasionally. Transfer peppers into a bowl, cover with plastic wrap, and steam for thirty minutes. Seed and skin peppers without rinsing, and reserve.

Scatter fennel seeds into a medium-sized *rondeau, and place over a medium-low flame. Shake pan frequently until aroma is released.

Adjust flame to low, and add a small amount of oil to film pan. Add onion, thyme, and garlic, season with pepper, and *sweat. Stir in peppers, bay leaf, stock, and tomato sauce. Bring mixture to the boil, reduce flame to low, and simmer for forty-five minutes.

While soup is simmering pour cream into a one quart saucepan. Reduce volume by half over a medium flame whisking often.

Remove bay leaf, cool soup slightly, and purée until smooth.

Pour soup into *rondeau, and whisk in reduced cream. Simmer briefly to develop flavor; lightly season to taste.

Plating:

Ladle red pepper cream into warmed deep bowls, and garnish with a pinch of parsley.

Yield:

four servings

*small dice: to cut to 1/4-inch square

*rondeau: a shallow, wide, straight-sided pot with handles

*sweat: to cook without color in a small amount of fat over a low flame

Chicken Stock

15 pounds chicken bones, well rinsed

1 1/2 large Spanish onion, *medium dice*

2 stalks celery, *medium dice*

1 1/2 carrot, *medium dice*

2 *sachet d' épices* tied in cheesecloth (3 parsley stems, 1/2 teaspoon dried thyme, 1 clove garlic, peeled, 1 bay leaf, and 3 black peppercorns *per* sachet)

Procedure:

Divide bones between two large stockpots, and fill with cold water to cover bones by two inches. Bring to the boil, and reduce to a simmer. Skim and discard impurities from the surface. Add vegetables and *sachet d' épices*. Simmer stock for four hours.

Place two large strainers over large stainless bowls, and strain stock. Press on solids to extract all juices; discard solids.

Quickly cool stock. Refrigerate overnight.

Remove fat cap, and discard. Divide stock between one quart containers, label, cover, and refrigerate. Use within forty-eight hours or freeze.

Yield:

five quarts

medium dice: to cut to 1/3-inch square

sachet d' épices: a small bag of aromatic spices

Cream of Carrot-Ginger Soup

1 ounce unsalted butter

1/2 small Spanish onion, *small dice*

1/3 leek, white part only, well-rinsed and *small dice*

3 cups carrots, sliced

3 tablespoons ginger, grated

48 ounces **Chicken Stock** (see recipe for **Chicken Stock**, page 35)

8 ounces heavy cream

salt and white pepper, to taste

granulated sugar, to taste

chervil sprigs, to garnish

Procedure:

Heat a small *rondeau* over a low flame, add butter to melt. Add onion, leek, and carrots; *sweat* vegetables. Stir in ginger, and cook briefly to release aroma. Add stock, and bring to the boil. Reduce flame to low, and simmer thirty minutes. Skim and discard surface impurities. Pour cream into a small saucepan, and warm over a low flame.

Place a sieve over a medium-sized bowl, and strain soup; reserve liquid and vegetables separately. Purée vegetables until very smooth adding liquid as needed. Rinse *rondeau*, and pour in purée. Steadily whisk in liquid to fully incorporate. Place *rondeau* over a medium flame, whisk in warmed cream, and cook to develop flavor. Adjust seasoning to taste.

Plating:

Pour soup into warmed deep bowls. Float a sprig of chervil to garnish.

Yield:

five servings

small dice: to cut to 1/4-inch square

rondeau: a shallow, wide, straight-sided pot with handles

sweat: to cook without color in a small amount of fat over a low flame

Chicken Consommé

2 ounces carrots, chopped

4 ounces leek, light green part only, well-rinsed and chopped

2 ounces celery, chopped

1/2 pound chicken thigh, raw, boneless, skinless and chopped

1 tablespoon fresh lemon juice

1 small bay leaf

1/4 teaspoon black peppercorns, crushed

1 sprig thyme

5 ounces egg whites, cold

5 quarts fresh **Chicken Stock**, cold (see recipe for **Chicken Stock**, page 35)

salt and white pepper, to taste

1/2 stalk peeled celery, *julienne*

12 enoki mushroom caps, rinsed

chives, minced, to garnish

Procedure:

Add carrots, leek, and celery into food processor work bowl fitted with metal blade; process until finely chopped. Add chicken, lemon juice, bay leaf, peppercorns, and thyme, and process to a purée. Scrape mixture into a medium-sized bowl. Using a rubber spatula, gradually stir in egg whites until evenly combined. This is the *raft.

Cover *raft, and refrigerate for one hour.

Pour stock into a straight-sided stockpot, place over a very low flame, and heat to a temperature of 80°. Stir in *raft to combine. Adjust flame to medium. Stir mixture every five minutes just until it reaches the boil. The *raft will coagulate and rise to the top.

Adjust flame to simmer consommé. Poke a hole in the center of the *raft. Carefully skim and discard impurities from the surface without disturbing the *raft. Simmer for forty-five minutes.

Rinse a double-thick square of cheesecloth in hot water, and wring out. Place cheesecloth over a fine sieve, and set over a smaller stockpot; carefully ladle consommé through sieve.

Bring consommé to a simmer, and season lightly.

Plating:

Place three enoki, and a pinch of celery and chives into the center of warmed deep bowls. Ladle consommé over vegetables.

Yield:

four servings

*julienne: to thinly slice to long, thin 1/8-inch rectangular strips

*raft: ingredients to clarify consommé that rise and float at the surface

Borscht

1 1/2 ounce refined sunflower oil

1 medium Spanish onion cut in eighths

3 medium carrots cut in eighths

1 large parsnip cut in eighths

1 celery stalk cut in eighths

6 small beets, trimmed, rinsed and divided

24 ounces cold water

3/4 ounce balsamic vinegar

fresh lemon juice, salt, and granulated sugar, to taste

sour cream, as needed

Procedure:

Preheat radiant oven to 400°. Peel and cut 2 beets in eighths, and combine with oil, onion, carrots, parsnip, and celery in a small roasting pan. Wrap 4 beets in foil, and place into a pie tin. Roast vegetables until lightly caramelized, turning frequently; roast beets until tender when pierced. Scrape caramelized vegetables into a small soup pot; add water and vinegar, and bring to the boil. Reduce flame, and simmer for forty-five minutes. Slightly cool beets and peel. Place a *mandoline over a small bowl, and *julienne beets. Cover, and refrigerate.

Strain stock into a medium-sized stainless bowl. Press on vegetables to release juices; discard vegetables, and season stock to taste. Place over an ice bath, undisturbed, until cold. Remove, and discard congealed fat.

Plating:

Place beets into cold bowls, and cover with stock. Scoop a mound of sour cream into center of borscht.

Yield:

four servings

*julienne: to thinly slice to long, thin 1/8-inch strips

*mandoline: a stainless slicer with blades adjustable for cut and thickness

୬

Baby Beet, Arugula, and Hazelnut Salad
~hazelnut vinaigrette

Hazelnut Vinaigrette

2 small cloves garlic, minced

1 teaspoon Grey Poupon® Dijon mustard

1 ounce red wine vinegar

2 ounces hazelnut oil

1 ounce safflower oil

salt, and freshly ground black pepper, to taste

Baby Beet, Arugula, and Hazelnut Salad

1/4 cup hazelnuts

2 baby beets with leaf greens

salt, as needed

2 ounces arugula

freshly ground black pepper, to taste

2 tablespoons chives, minced

Procedure for Hazelnut Vinaigrette:

Place garlic, Dijon, and vinegar into food processor work bowl fitted with steel blade, and process to combine. Combine oils. With machine running, slowly add oils to emulsify; adjust seasoning. Pour into a lidded jar, cover, and refrigerate.

Procedure for Baby Beet, Arugula, and Hazelnut Salad:

Preheat radiant oven to 350°. Pour hazelnuts onto a parchment-lined baking sheet. Bake nuts until lightly golden brown. Pour onto a thin towel, and rub to remove skin. Cool, and coarsely chop nuts.

Rinse, and trim beets. Place into a small saucepan, cover with cold water, and season lightly with salt. Bring to the boil, reduce flame to low, and simmer until tender, approximately forty minutes.

Rinse, and spin-dry beet greens and arugula; *chiffonade*, and combine in a medium-sized bowl. Cover with a dampened tea towel, and refrigerate. Drain beets, cool slightly, peel and *small dice*. Place into a small bowl, and refrigerate.

Plating:

Season greens, and dress lightly with vinaigrette; toss to coat. Dress beets lightly with vinaigrette. Pile greens high on four cold plates, and mound beets in center. Scatter hazelnuts and chives.

Yield:

four servings

chiffonade: to finely julienne

small dice: to cut to 1/4-inch square

Spinach and Feta Cheese Salad
~calamata olive dressing

Calamata Olive Dressing

1 large egg, room temperature

1 large clove garlic, chopped

1 small shallot, chopped

2 teaspoons capers, rinsed

1 tablespoon parsley, chopped

1/4 cup Calamata olives, pitted, chopped and well-drained

freshly ground black pepper, as needed

1 1/2 teaspoon Grey Poupon® Dijon mustard

1 ounce champagne vinegar

4 ounces canola oil

salt, to taste

Spinach and Feta Cheese Salad

4 ounces baby spinach, rinsed and spin-dried

2 ounces scallions, white part only, thinly sliced

3 ounces radishes, thinly sliced

4 ounces grape tomatoes, halved

3 ounces Feta, rinsed, drained and crumbled

2 hard-boiled eggs, grated

Procedure for Calamata Olive Dressing:

Fill a small bowl with ice and water. Fill a small saucepan with water, place over a medium flame, and bring to a simmer. Gently place egg, and *coddle* for two minutes. *Shock* in ice bath. Separate yolk and white; discard egg white. Place garlic, shallot, capers, parsley, and olives into food processor work bowl fitted with metal blade, season with black pepper; process until minced. Add yolk and Dijon; process to emulsify scraping frequently. Add vinegar; process to combine. With machine running, slowly add oil to emulsify. Season; pour into a lidded jar, cover, and refrigerate.

Procedure for Spinach and Feta Cheese Salad:

Place spinach, scallions and radishes into a medium-sized bowl; cover with a dampened tea towel, and refrigerate.

Plating:

Dress spinach mixture lightly, and toss to coat. Add tomatoes, and Feta; toss. Mound salad on four cold plates, and sprinkle with grated eggs.

Yield:

four servings

coddle: to cook in water just below the boiling point

shock: to stop the cooking process

Asparagus, Vermont Blue, and Mâche
~blue cheese vinaigrette

Blue Cheese Vinaigrette

1 clove garlic, minced

1 teaspoon shallot, minced

1/4 teaspoon Grey Poupon® Dijon mustard

1 ounce champagne vinegar

1 teaspoon Worcestershire sauce

3/4 ounce Vermont blue cheese, cold

3 ounces peanut oil

dash salt and 1/4 teaspoon freshly ground black pepper

Asparagus, Vermont Blue, and Mâche

16 thin asparagus spears

4 ounces mâche, rinsed and spin-dried

2 ounces Vermont blue cheese, crumbled

Procedure for Blue Cheese Vinaigrette:

Place garlic, shallot, Dijon, vinegar, and Worcestershire sauce into food processor work bowl fitted with steel blade, and combine; scrape bowl. Crumble 3/4 ounce blue cheese over mixture. With machine running, slowly add oil to emulsify; scrape bowl. Add seasonings, and pulse to combine. Pour into a lidded jar, cover, and refrigerate.

Procedure for Asparagus:

Trim and peel ends of asparagus. Half fill a medium-sized bowl with ice and water. Three-fourths fill a ten inch skillet with water, season liberally with salt, and bring to a simmer over a low flame. *Blanch* asparagus until emerald green. *Shock* in ice bath, drain, and pat dry.

Plating:

Stir vinaigrette. Divide mâche between four chilled glass plates. Scatter greens with blue cheese. Crisscross asparagus over mâche, and drizzle vinaigrette.

Yield:

four servings

blanch: to cook briefly in boiling water or hot fat

shock: to stop the cooking process

Spring Greens
~maple-balsamic vinaigrette

Maple-Balsamic Vinaigrette

> 3/4 ounce pure Vermont maple syrup
>
> 3/4 ounce balsamic vinegar
>
> 1 ounce dry white wine
>
> 2 teaspoons shallots, minced
>
> 1/4 teaspoon Coleman's® dry mustard
>
> 1 1/3 ounce peanut oil
>
> 1 1/2 ounce safflower oil
>
> 1/2 ounce olive oil
>
> dash salt

Salad

6 ounces spring greens (baby spinach and lettuces, arugula, cress, mâche, and torn mustard, dandelion, radish, and beet leaves)

> salt, and freshly ground black pepper to taste

Procedure for Maple-Balsamic Vinaigrette:

Pour maple syrup, balsamic vinegar, white wine, shallots, and dry mustard into food processor work bowl fitted with metal blade; process until blended. Combine oils. With machine running, slowly add oil to emulsify, and season lightly. Pour into a lidded jar, cover, and refrigerate.

Procedure for Salad:

Rinse and spin-dry spring greens. Place into a medium-sized bowl; cover with a dampened tea towel, and refrigerate.

Plating:

Season greens, and dress lightly with vinaigrette; toss to coat. Pile salad high on cold glass plates.

Yield:

four servings

**Dressed Brook Trout stuffed with Bell Pepper Pesto
~red wine sauce steamed spinach and shallots**

Red Wine Sauce

8 ounces soft red wine

2 shallots, chopped

3 cloves garlic, chopped

2 bay leaves

3 sprigs thyme

1/2 tablespoon black peppercorns

1/2 lemon, juiced

8 ounces **Veal Stock** (recipe follows **Dressed Brook Trout**)

salt, to taste

1/2 ounce port wine

1 ounce unsalted butter, cold

Pesto-stuffed Brook Trout

10 small cloves garlic, peeled

1 small red bell pepper

olive oil, as needed

1/2 cup pine nuts, lightly toasted

2 tablespoons basil leaves, *chiffonade*

1/2 ounce extra virgin olive oil

salt and white pepper, as needed

4 *dressed* wild brook trout

3 ounces unbleached all purpose flour

olive oil, as needed

Spinach and Shallots

olive oil, as needed

2 shallots, minced

freshly ground black pepper, as needed

15 ounces leaf spinach, stemmed (weight after stemming)

salt, as needed

Procedure for Red Wine Sauce:

Pour wine into a one quart saucepan. Add shallots, garlic, bay leaves, thyme, peppercorns, and lemon juice. Bring mixture to the boil, adjust flame to medium-low, and reduce volume to four tablespoons. Add veal stock, and continue to cook until slightly thickened and volume is reduced by half. Skim and discard impurities from surface.

Pour sauce through a sieve into a small stainless bowl; press on solids to extract juices. Discard solids. Season sauce lightly, and whisk in port and butter. Cover bowl with plastic wrap, and place over a saucepan of barely simmering water.

Procedure for Pesto-stuffed Brook Trout:

Preheat radiant oven to 400°. Keep oven on throughout procedure.

Place garlic and red pepper into a small pan, and lightly rub with oil. Roast vegetables until garlic is golden and pepper is lightly charred turning occasionally. Remove garlic, and hold aside. Place pepper into a small bowl, and cover with plastic wrap. Allow pepper to steam for twenty minutes.

Skin and seed pepper without rinsing. Place pepper and garlic into food processor work bowl fitted with metal blade. Add pine nuts and basil, and pulse on and off until roughly chopped. With machine running, add extra virgin olive oil in a steady stream; season to taste. Do *not* process to a paste: texture should be retained.

Lightly season the flesh of trout, and stuff with pesto. Pour flour into a pie tin. Lightly dredge trout. Discard unused flour.

Place two, ten inch sauté pans over a medium flame. Generously film pans with oil, and heat. Quickly *pan-fry* trout until golden on one side; flip trout, and place pans into oven. Roast trout until flesh is opaque and firm to the touch approximately twelve to fifteen minutes.

Procedure for Spinach and Shallots:

Rinse, drain, and spin-dry spinach. Heat a large *rondeau* over a low flame. Film pan with oil, add shallots and a little black pepper; *sweat.* Adjust flame to high, stir in spinach and a little salt; cover and steam for one minute, or until barely wilted. Remove from heat.

Plating:

Center spinach on four large warmed plates. Place trout on top of spinach, and encircle entrée with drizzled sauce.

Yield:

four servings

chiffonade: to finely julienne

dressed: to gut, scale, debone, and remove fins, head and tail of fish

pan-fry: to cook coated food in a skillet of hot oil over a medium flame

rondeau: a shallow, wide, straight-sided pot with handles

sweat: to cook without color in a small amount of fat over a low flame

Veal Stock

7 pounds veal bones

olive oil, as needed

4 ounces tomato paste

1 large Spanish onion, *medium dice*

2 carrots, *medium dice*

2 stalks celery, *medium dice*

cold water, as needed

sachet d' épices tied in cheesecloth (3 parsley stems, 1/2 teaspoon dried thyme,

1 clove garlic, peeled, 1 bay leaf, and 3 black peppercorns)

4 ounces dry red wine

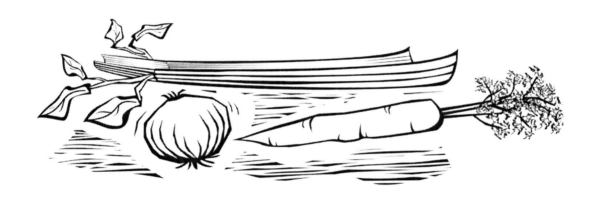

Procedure:

Preheat radiant oven to 450°.

Place bones, single layer, into a roasting pan, and rub lightly with oil. Roast bones until deeply caramelized; turn bones. Spread tomato paste over bones, and scatter with vegetables. Continue to roast until vegetables are golden brown.

Pour bone mixture into a large stockpot. Add cold water to cover four inches above bones.

Place roasting pan over two burners, and adjust flame to medium; add wine and bring to a low boil, scraping pan constantly. Reduce liquid to two tablespoons, and add to stockpot.

Bring mixture to the boil, and immediately adjust flame to low. Skim and discard surface impurities. Add *sachet d' épices. Simmer stock for six hours.

Pour stock through a strainer into a large stainless bowl. Remove bones, and place onto a baking sheet to cool. Press solids to extract all juices. Discard solids.

Quickly cool stock. Refrigerate overnight.

Wrap bones; label, and freeze for *remouillage.

Remove fat cap from stock. Portion into half-quart containers; label, cover, and refrigerate. Use within forty eight hours, or freeze.

Yield:

three quarts

*medium dice: to cut to 1/3-inch square

*sachet d' épices: a small packet of aromatic spices

*remouillage: a secondary stock prepared with the bones used to prepare a stock

Lamb Chop and Fava Bean Ragoût
~whipped potatoes

1 1/2 pound fresh fava beans

salt, as needed

olive oil, as needed

4, 6-ounce blade lamb chops

freshly ground black pepper, as needed

2 medium Spanish onions, *small dice*

3 carrots, *small dice*

4 small cloves garlic, minced

2 tablespoons tomato paste

3 ounces dry red wine

cold water, as needed

1 bay leaf

1/2 cup Picholine olives, pitted and halved

1 tablespoon fresh thyme leaves, chopped

1 medium Roma tomato, seeded and *small dice*

Whipped Potatoes (recipe follows **Lamb Chop and Fava Beans Ragoût**)

parsley, finely chopped, to garnish

Procedure:

Half fill a four and one-half quart saucepan with water, season with salt, and bring to the boil. Add beans; *blanch for one minute, and drain. Rinse with cold water; drain. Slash pods, and pop out beans. Refrigerate beans, and discard pods.

Heat a large *rondeau over a medium-high flame, and film with oil. Season lamb; add to *rondeau, and *sear. Transfer into a bowl, and reserve.

Adjust flame to medium-low, add additional oil as needed. Stir in onions, carrots, and garlic, season with black pepper, and cook until vegetables are lightly caramelized stirring occasionally. Add tomato paste, and cook for five minutes. Adjust flame to high, add wine, and reduce until syrupy stirring constantly. Add lamb and accumulated juices, and cold water to just cover chops. Add bay leaf, and bring to the boil. Adjust flame to low, partially cover *rondeau, and *braise until lamb is fork-tender fifty minutes to one hour. Skim and discard surface impurities. Add water as needed to keep chops nearly covered. Remove cooked lamb. Discard bay leaf.

Stir in fava beans, olives, thyme, and tomato. Increase flame to medium, and cook until beans are tender. Adjust consistency and seasoning as needed. Turn flame to low, immerse lamb, and heat through.

Plating:

Mound whipped potatoes into four warmed deep bowls. Lean chops against potatoes, and ladle generously with sauce and vegetables. Garnish with chopped parsley.

Yield:

four servings

*small dice: to cut to 1/4-inch square

*blanch: to cook briefly in boiling water or hot fat

*rondeau: a shallow, wide, straight-sided pot with handles

*sear: to brown the surface of food in fat over a high flame

*braise: to simmer partially covered in stock or another liquid

Whipped Potatoes

2 pounds waxy potatoes, peeled and *large dice* (weight after peeling)

salt, as needed

4 ounces unsalted butter

10 ounces heavy cream

white pepper, to taste

Procedure:

Pour potatoes into a six quart pot, and cover with cold water by two inches. Bring to the boil, and salt the water to taste the salt. Cook potatoes until tender yet not falling apart.

Place butter and heavy cream into a small saucepan. Heat until butter melts over a medium-low flame.

Drain potatoes thoroughly. Pour into a 5-quart KitchenAid® mixer bowl, and attach flat beater. Beat potatoes on speed 2 until smooth.

Replace flat beater with whip, and turn to speed 2. Steadily add hot cream and butter while increasing speed; whip until fluffy. Adjust seasoning, and whip briefly.

Yield:

one quart

large dice: to cut to 3/4-inch square

Poached Turbot with Tomato-Herb Broth

14 ounces cold water, divided

14 ounces dry white wine, divided

1 tablespoon shallot, minced

olive oil, as needed

1 large carrot, *brunoise*

1 medium Spanish onion, *brunoise*

3 tablespoons scallions, white part only, thinly sliced

1 teaspoon garlic, minced

dash cayenne

1 teaspoon Better than Bouillon® lobster base

3 ounces brandy

2 tablespoons tomato paste

1 pound Roma tomatoes, *small dice*

salt and white pepper, as needed

4, 6-ounce hand-line turbot steaks

unsalted butter, as needed

2 tablespoons scallion greens, thinly sliced

2 tablespoons parsley, finely chopped

1 tablespoon chervil, finely chopped

Procedure:

Pour 6 ounces each of cold water and wine into a ten inch skillet, and stir in shallot. Bring liquids to barely a simmer over a medium flame.

Heat another ten inch skillet over a low flame and film with oil. Add carrot, onion, scallions, and garlic, season with cayenne, and *sweat* vegetables.

Pour 8 ounces cold water into a small saucepan, and bring to the boil. Stir in lobster base. Remove from heat, and reserve.

Adjust flame under skillet of vegetables to medium-high; add brandy, and *flambé*. When flames extinguish reduce until syrupy stirring constantly. Whisk in tomato paste, 8 ounces wine, and lobster broth, and bring to the boil. Adjust flame to low, and simmer to develop flavor. Add tomatoes. Lightly season tomato broth with salt, and hold warm over a very low flame.

Preheat radiant oven to 350°.

Scantly season turbot steaks with salt and white pepper; butter a 10-inch parchment circle on one side only.

Place turbot into skillet of simmering water and wine. Adjust flame to bring liquid quickly to the boil. Press parchment circle buttered side down against fish. Place skillet into oven, and poach turbot until flesh is creamy white and firm approximately fifteen minutes.

Plating:

Place turbot steaks into four large warmed bowls. Stir scallion greens and herbs into tomato broth, and ladle over fish.

Yield:

four servings

brunoise: to cut to 1/8-inch square

small dice: to cut to 1/4-inch square

sweat: to cook without color in a small amount of fat over a low flame

flambé: to pour spirits over food and ignite

Chicken Roulade of Prosciutto, Asparagus, and Havarti
~morel cream sauce, fiddleheads, and russet potato

Crème Fraîche

1 cup heavy cream

1 tablespoon buttermilk, fresh and well-shaken

Roulade

salt, as needed

8 asparagus spears, trimmed to 3-inch lengths

4, 4-ounce chicken breasts, boneless and skinless

freshly ground black pepper, as needed

4 slices prosciutto, thinly sliced

4 slices Havarti, thinly sliced

4 ounces Parmigiano Reggiano, finely grated

3 ounces unbleached all purpose flour

refined sunflower oil, as needed

pan spray, as needed

Morel Cream Sauce

3/4 ounce dried morel mushrooms

12 ounces **Chicken Stock** (see recipe for **Chicken Stock**, page 35)

3 tablespoons shallots, minced

1 teaspoon garlic, minced

freshly ground black pepper, as needed

2 ounces marsala wine

1/2 tablespoon thyme leaves, chopped

3/4 cup crème fraîche (see Procedure)

dash cayenne

salt, to taste

Accompaniments

4 ounces fiddleheads, evenly trimmed

1 ounce cold water and 1 tablespoon unsalted butter

salt, to taste

4 russet potatoes, baked and hot

crème fraîche, as needed

chives, minced, as needed

Procedure for Crème Fraîche:

Combine heavy cream and buttermilk by stirring in a clean glass jar with a lid. Place in a warm space in the kitchen, lidded and undisturbed, for thirty-six hours. Lightly whisk to serve.

Refrigerate crème fraîche. It will continue to thicken and will remain fresh for one week.

Procedure for Roulades and Fiddleheads:

Half fill a medium-sized bowl with ice and water. Fill a ten inch skillet three-fourths full with cold water, season to taste the salt, and bring to barely a simmer over a medium flame. *Blanch* asparagus until emerald green. *Shock* in ice bath, lift out, towel-dry and reserve. Soak fiddleheads in cold water to release dirt. Lift out, and rinse brown flaky casings from tender shoots. *Blanch* fiddleheads until tender. *Shock*, drain, and place into a lidded container. Cover, and refrigerate.

Place each chicken breast between two large sheets of plastic wrap; pound to 1/4-inch thickness using the flat side of a meat mallet. Remove top sheet of plastic wrap, and discard. Scantly season chicken; cover each breast with one slice of prosciutto. Trim Havarti slice to fit the center of each breast, and place on top of prosciutto. Place two spears of asparagus on either side of each Havarti slice. Sprinkle breasts evenly with Parmigiano Reggiano.

Roll each breast into a tight cylinder in the plastic wrap, and twist the ends to seal. Refrigerate roulades until cold.

Procedure for Morel Cream Sauce and Cooking Roulades:

Place morels into a small saucepan, and cover with stock. Bring to the boil, cover, and remove from heat. Allow morels to steep for twenty minutes. Strain through a fine sieve placed over a small bowl. *Julienne morels; reserve broth and mushrooms separately.

Preheat radiant oven to 350°.

Pour 3 ounces flour into a pie tin. Lightly dredge roulades; discard unused flour. Heat a ten inch cast-iron skillet over a medium flame, and generously film with oil. Un-wrap roulades, place seam side down into skillet, and evenly brown turning frequently. Pan spray a small baking sheet. Place roulades seam side down on baking sheet, and roast until flesh is cooked approximately fifteen minutes.

Return cast-iron skillet to stove, and place over a low flame. Add morels, shallots, and garlic, season with black pepper, and *sweat. Increase flame to medium-high, add marsala and reduce until syrupy stirring constantly. Stir in morel broth and thyme, bring to the boil, adjust fame to medium and reduce to a thin sauce consistency. Whisk in crème fraîche. Cook to develop consistency and depth of flavor whisking occasionally. Season with cayenne and salt, and remove from heat.

Pour 1 ounce cold water and 1 tablespoon butter into a ten inch sauté pan, and bring to the boil. Add fiddleheads, season lightly, and toss until hot and liquid evaporates.

Plating:

Diagonally slice each roulade. Ladle morel sauce onto right half of four large warmed plates. Overlap roulade slices over sauce forming a half circle. Scatter fiddleheads on left half, and center potato lengthwise. Slit potato, mound with crème fraîche, and sprinkle with chives.

Yield:

four servings

*blanch: to cook briefly in boiling water or hot fat

*shock: to stop the cooking process

*julienne: to thinly slice to long, thin 1/8-inch rectangular strips

*sweat: to cook without color in a small amount of fat over a low flame

Pistachio Sponge Cake with Mascarpone Cheese Frosting
~chocolate sauce

Biscuit

pan spray, as needed

2 ounces and 1 cup unsalted pistachios, divided

8 large egg yolks, room temperature

1 cup superfine sugar, divided

1 1/2 teaspoon vanilla extract

1 teaspoon lemon zest, minced

4 ounces sifted cake flour

8 large egg whites, room temperature

dash salt

1 teaspoon cream of tartar

Lemon Syrup

3 ounces granulated sugar

4 ounces water

4 teaspoons fresh lemon juice

Mascarpone Cheese Frosting

8 ounces heavy cream

1/4 cup granulated sugar, divided

1 teaspoon vanilla extract

1/2 pound cream cheese, room temperature

1 pound Vermont mascarpone cheese, cold

Chocolate Sauce

3 1/2 ounces Callebault® semisweet chocolate, chopped

1 1/2 ounce unsalted butter, softened

1 1/2 ounce water, room temperature

Procedure for Biscuit:

Preheat radiant oven to 350°. Pan spray the bottom of two 8 x 2-inch cake pans, and line with 8-inch parchment circles.

Pour all of pistachios onto a parchment-lined baking sheet. Bake nuts for eight minutes. Pour onto a thin towel, and rub vigorously to remove skins. Cool pistachios; very finely chop 2 ounces. Chop remaining pistachios, and reserve for decorating cake.

Pour yolks and 3/4 cup superfine sugar into a KitchenAid® 5-quart mixer bowl, and attach whip. Whip on high speed until mixture nearly triples in volume, and is pale yellow. Add vanilla, and whip briefly. Scatter finely chopped pistachios and zest over mixture.

Pour flour into a sifter placed over a small plate. Steadily and evenly sift and fold flour and pistachios into yolk mixture.

Pour whites into a clean 5-quart KitchenAid® mixer bowl, add salt and cream of tartar, and attach whip. Turn speed to 4, and whip whites until foamy. Steadily increase speed while adding remaining 1/4 cup superfine sugar. Whip to a satiny firm meringue—mixture should peak, and gently fall back when whip is lifted.

Fold one-third of meringue into yolk and flour mixture using a large balloon whisk. Gently and thoroughly fold in remaining meringue with a rubber spatula.

Pour into prepared pans, gently level batter, and place on a baking sheet.

Bake approximately thirty minutes, or until biscuit is golden brown, and center springs back when lightly touched.

Place pans on cooling racks. Guide a thin paring knife between biscuit and pan to loosen cake. Place a parchment circle onto each cake, and invert on cooling racks. Remove pans, and peel off parchment. Re-invert, remove parchment, and cool completely.

Remove the thin golden top crust from biscuit with a long, thin serrated knife. Slice each cake into two layers, and cover with a tea towel.

Procedure for Lemon Syrup:

Pour sugar and water into a small saucepan, and bring to the boil. Remove from heat; stir in lemon juice, and reserve.

Procedure for Mascarpone Cheese Frosting and Assembling Cake:

Place 5-quart KitchenAid® mixer bowl and whip into refrigerator until cold.

Pour cream into cold bowl, and whip on medium speed until cream begins to hold shape. Sprinkle in 1 tablespoon sugar and vanilla extract, and continue to whip without graininess to firm peak. Do *not* over whip. Refrigerate.

Place cream cheese into a 5-quart KitchenAid® mixer bowl, and attach flat beater. Beat cheese on speed 2 until very smooth; steadily add remaining sugar, and beat until thoroughly combined.

Fold mascarpone into cream cheese mixture just until combined. Fold in approximately one-fourth of whipped cream to lighten density. Gently and thoroughly fold in remaining whipped cream.

Place one layer of biscuit on a 9-inch cake circle. Brush top and sides with lemon syrup, and spread an even layer of frosting. Repeat procedure with remaining layers. Frost cake, and decorate with reserved chopped pistachios and piped frosting borders. Refrigerate cake until cold.

Procedure for Chocolate Sauce:

Pour chocolate into a small stainless bowl, and place over a saucepan of simmering water. Melt chocolate. Stir butter into chocolate with a rubber spatula. Steadily stir in water until sauce is smooth and shiny. Turn off flame.

Plating:

Slice cake using a long, thin serrated knife. Drizzle chocolate sauce lightly onto glass plates. Place cake slice over sauce.

Yield:

eight servings

Strawberry Charlotte Russe
~strawberry sauce

2 pounds fresh strawberries, stemmed

10 3/4 ounces granulated sugar, divided

1 tablespoon orange zest, minced

20 ounces heavy cream, divided

1 teaspoon vanilla extract

4 3/4 ounces cold water, divided

1 tablespoon Triple Sec liquor

2 1/2 teaspoons gelatin

4 large egg yolks, room temperature

25 ladyfingers

Strawberry Sauce (see Procedure)

Procedure:

Line a 6-cup charlotte mold with plastic wrap, smooth out creases and leave an overhang.

Choose 8 equally sized strawberries, and thinly slice from point to stem. Arrange half of the sliced berries in concentric circles onto bottom of mold, with points of berries turned toward the sides of mold. Reserve the remaining sliced berries.

Roughly chop 1 pound of strawberries, and place into a medium-sized bowl. Sprinkle 4 ounces sugar over berries, add zest, and combine. Allow berries to soften at room temperature stirring occasionally; *small dice* remaining strawberries, and reserve.

Refrigerate a medium-sized stainless bowl and a whisk until very cold. Pour 12 ounces heavy cream into cold bowl, and whisk until it begins to thicken. Steadily add 1 1/4 ounce sugar and vanilla extract, and whisk until quite thickened yet still pourable. Refrigerate cream.

Combine 2 ounces water and 1 ounce sugar in a small saucepan, and bring to the boil. Remove from heat, and stir in Triple Sec. Reserve Tripe Sec syrup.

Pour 2 3/4 ounces cold water into a small pan, and sprinkle with gelatin. Allow gelatin to soften.

Pour 8 ounces heavy cream into a small saucepan, and bring to the boil. Pour yolks and 3 ounces sugar into a medium-sized bowl, and whisk until thickened and pale yellow. Steadily whisk boiled cream into yolks to *temper*. Pour yolk mixture into saucepan, and stir constantly over a low flame until custard slightly thickens. Pour custard into a medium-sized stainless bowl.

Place pan of gelatin over a very low flame, and stir until melted. Stir into custard.

Purée softened strawberries. Stir 1 cup of purée into custard, and refrigerate for fifteen minutes. Do *not* allow custard to set.

Fold one-fourth of whipped cream into custard. Fold all of custard and reserved *small dice* strawberries into whipped cream.

To make **strawberry sauce**, gradually stir 1 1/2 ounce sugar into remaining purée until dissolved. Pass through a sieve into a small bowl, cover, and refrigerate.

Trim ladyfingers to the height of charlotte mold. Tightly place next to one another around the mold, and brush with Triple Sec syrup. Pour in strawberry cream mixture to half fill the mold. Arrange reserved sliced strawberries in concentric circles with points of berries turned toward the sides of mold. Pour in remaining strawberry cream mixture to reach the top of the ladyfingers. Arrange a petal design on top using the remaining ladyfingers, and brush with Triple Sec syrup.

Cover charlotte with plastic wrap, and freeze for twenty-four hours.

Plating:

Invert charlotte onto a serving plate; remove and discard plastic wrap. Refrigerate charlotte for four hours. Slice using a warm, dry, thin knife. Center slice on a rimmed dessert plate, and ladle strawberry sauce over top.

Yield:

eight servings

small dice: to cut to 1/4-inch square

temper: to incorporate a hot liquid into an egg mixture to equalize temperature

White Chocolate and Maple Mousse in Almond Tuile

Mousse

10 ounces Callebaut® white chocolate, chopped

16 ounces heavy cream

4 ounces pure Vermont maple syrup

6.5 ounces pasteurized egg whites, room temperature

3/4 teaspoon cream of tartar

dash salt

2 ounces granulated sugar

Tuiles

2 3/4 ounces unsalted butter, softened

9 ounces confectioners' sugar, and additional for sifting

8 large egg whites, room temperature and lightly combined

3 3/4 ounces unbleached all purpose flour, and additional for dusting

dash salt

9 ounces sliced almonds, and additional to garnish, lightly toasted and chopped

pan spray, as needed

Procedure for Mousse:

Refrigerate a medium-sized stainless bowl and a whisk until very cold.

Pour heavy cream into cold bowl, and whip until cream begins to hold shape. Steadily add maple syrup, and continue to whip to firm peak without graininess. Do *not* over whip cream. Refrigerate.

Place chocolate into a flat-bottomed medium-sized stainless bowl. Place bowl over a saucepan of barely simmering water to completely melt. Stir to combine. Turn off flame.

Pour whites, cream of tartar, and salt into a 5-quart KitchenAid® mixer bowl, and attach whip. Turn mixer to speed 4, and whip whites until foamy. Steadily add sugar while increasing speed; whip to a satiny firm meringue—mixture should peak, and gently fall back when whip is lifted.

Gently and thoroughly fold one-third of meringue into warm chocolate with a rubber spatula. Fold in remaining meringue. Lightly whisk whipped cream. Gently fold one-half of whipped cream into chocolate-meringue mixture. Gently and thoroughly fold all of mixture into remaining whipped cream.

Cover mousse with plastic wrap, and refrigerate.

Procedure for Tuiles:

Place butter and confectioners' sugar into a small stainless bowl, and cream mixture using a wooden spoon. Gradually stir in egg whites, incorporating each addition.

Place sifter on a plate, and pour in flour and salt; sift steadily over egg white mixture while stirring to combine. Fold in 9 ounces almonds.

Preheat radiant oven to 375°.

Pan spray two flat baking sheets, and dust with flour.

Set out four small soup cups without handles for shaping tuiles.

Spread 2 tablespoons of batter, per cookie, into a thin even circle on a prepared baking sheet. Prepare two cookies per baking sheet. Bake cookies for eight minutes or until edges are lightly golden brown.

Using a small thin spatula quickly remove one cookie, and press firmly over one soup cup, fluting edges. Repeat with second cookie pressed over another soup cup.

Prepare two more cookies on the second baking sheet; bake, and press cookies onto remaining soup cups. Remove cooled cookies from cups to a cooling rack.

Wash cooled baking sheets, pan spray, and dust with flour. Repeat the entire procedure until twelve tuiles are prepared, (amount allows for breakage). Cover, and refrigerate any unused batter.

Serve tuiles within hours of baking.

Plating:

Lightly sift confectioners' sugar over colorful dessert plates. Place one tuile in the center of each plate. Using a warm, dry kitchen spoon mound a large scoop of mousse inside tuile. Garnish with sliced almonds.

Yield:

eight servings

Key Lime Tartlets
~fruit salsa

Tartlets

1 recipe **Pâte Brisée** rolled to 1/8-inch thickness, and refrigerated
(see recipe for **Pâte Brisée**, page 24)

unsalted butter, as needed

pastry flour, as needed

1 egg combined with 1 tablespoon cold water for egg wash

6 ounces heavy cream

1 1/2 teaspoon granulated sugar

3 ounces cold water

3/4 tablespoon gelatin

4 large eggs, room temperature

8 ounces sweetened condensed milk

6 ounces Key lime or Mexican lime juice, freshly squeezed

1 1/2 teaspoon lime zest, minced

Fruit Salsa

1 ounce cold water

2 ounces granulated sugar

1 1/2 ounce tangerine juice, freshly squeezed

1/4 teaspoon Key lime or Mexican lime juice, freshly squeezed

1/4 cup strawberries, *small dice*

1/4 cup kiwi, peeled and *small dice*

1/4 cup tangerine segments, peeled and *small dice*

1/4 teaspoon lime zest, minced

Procedure for Tartlets:

Butter six 4 1/2-inch tartlet pans. Place rolled pâte brisée on a lightly floured work surface. Cut out six 5 1/2-inch rounds from dough and gently form into prepared pans, reinforce sides. Place tartlet shells on a baking sheet, and refrigerate for thirty minutes.

Preheat radiant oven to 375°. Prick sides and bottoms of shells with a fork. Line each tartlet shell with a 6-inch circle of waxed paper, and fill with beans. Bake shells for twenty minutes, and remove from oven. Remove waxed paper and beans, and brush lightly with egg wash. Place baking sheet into oven, and bake shells briefly until golden brown.

Cool shells completely on a rack. Remove rims and bottoms of tartlet pans.

Refrigerate a medium-sized stainless bowl and a whisk until very cold. Pour heavy cream into bowl, and whip until cream begins to hold shape. Steadily add sugar, and continue whipping until nearly firm peak. Do *not* over whip. Refrigerate.

Pour 3 ounces cold water into a small pan, and sprinkle with gelatin. Allow gelatin to soften.

Fill a small stainless bowl with ice and water. Half fill a two quart saucepan with water, place over a medium flame, and bring to a simmer. Gently place eggs, and *coddle* for two minutes. Immediately *shock* eggs in ice bath. Crack eggs, and separate the yolks from the whites. Discard whites.

Pour yolks, sweetened condensed milk, lime juice, and zest into a small bowl, and whisk to combine. Place pan of gelatin over a very low flame, and stir until melted. Stir into yolk mixture. Place shells on a baking sheet. Divide lime mixture evenly between shells.

Scrape whipped cream into a pastry bag fitted with a large open-star tip. Completely cover each tartlet with a piped rosette. Refrigerate tartlets until set, approximately four hours.

Procedure for Fruit Salsa:

Combine water, sugar, tangerine and lime juices in a small saucepan, and bring to the boil. Remove syrup from heat, and cool completely. Combine syrup, strawberries, kiwi, tangerine, and lime zest in a small bowl. Allow flavors to develop at room temperature for one hour. Strain fruit salsa over a small jar; drain thoroughly. Pour salsa into a small bowl. Cover, and refrigerate syrup for another use.

Plating:

Place tartlet on dessert plate. Mound a spoonful of salsa onto center of rosette.

Yield:

six tartlets

small dice: to cut to 1/4-inch square

coddle: to cook in water just below the boiling point

shock: to stop the cooking process

The Summer Season

A fragrant scent of freshly mowed hay wafts on a gentle breeze. The rollicking waves of crystal-clear waters bid Vermonters back to camp. Hikers and bicyclists cover miles of forested mountain trails, river walks, and scenic roadways. Well-trodden woodland paths lead locals to refreshingly cool, deep water swimming holes. It's summertime in Vermont.

Farm stand bins spill with fresh summer greens and scented herbs. A colorful array of garden vegetables—tomatoes, sweet corn, spinach, swiss chard, sorrel, garlic, onions, beans, broccoli, cauliflower, squash, beets, cucumbers, celery, carrots, eggplant, potatoes, peppers, peas, and California avocados—inspire our culinary creativity. The sun-ripened, juicy-sweet taste of summer berries and fruits tempts our appetite. Gooseberries, blueberries, raspberries, blackberries, currants, plums, and melons are irresistible. Although not indigenous, luscious peaches, nectarines, apricots, and sweet cherries are distinctively summertime.

The long, hot days of summer are ideal for outdoor dining. The smoky, slightly charred flavor of grilling complements the gardens' abounding fresh goodness.

Teriyaki-Marinated Tri-Tip Sirloin
~parmesan and gruyère whipped potatoes

Moist and juicy thin slices of grilled beef sirloin drizzled with pungent teriyaki jus are draped over sharp and nutty flavored creamy Parmesan and Gruyère whipped potatoes.

Ratatouille Salad with Fresh Buffalo Mozzarella

Garden-fresh vegetables redolent with the piquant perfume of onion, garlic, and black pepper, and the sweet-and-sour zing of ripened tomatoes are tossed with fresh mozzarella, and nested in delicately flavored Bibb lettuce petals.

Fresh Plum Tartlets
~black pepper-scented ice cream

Rich and juicy, sweet and tart purple plums are baked in a buttery encasement of hazelnut pastry and sweet toasty streusel. A lingering aromatic perfumes the rich flavor of ice cream, beguiling the senses.

Delicious.

સ્જ

Crab-Stuffed Chive Crêpe Pillows
~roasted corn cream

Chive Crêpes

125 grams all purpose flour, sifted

1/4 teaspoon salt

1 large egg, room temperature

1 large egg yolk, room temperature

1/2 ounce *clarified butter*

9 ounces whole milk, scalded and cooled

1 tablespoon fresh chives, minced

Roasted Corn Cream

1 ear corn

4 ounces heavy cream

Crab Stuffed Pillows

6 ounces canned hand-picked Blue crab meat, flaked

3 tablespoons roasted corn, chopped (see Procedure)

3 tablespoons carrot, *brunoise*

3 tablespoons celery, *brunoise*

1 tablespoon parsley, finely chopped

1 tablespoon fresh lemon juice

3 tablespoons fresh chives, minced and divided

2 ounces heavy cream

salt and white pepper, to taste

clarified butter, as needed

1/2 cup Monterey Jack, grated

Procedure for Chive Crêpes:

Combine flour and salt in a small stainless bowl.

Whisk egg, yolk, and 1 tablespoon *clarified butter* in another small bowl. Whisk in milk and chives to combine.

Gradually whisk wet ingredients into dry, thoroughly incorporating each addition. Cover bowl with plastic wrap. Allow batter to stand at room temperature for one hour.

Procedure for Roasted Corn Cream:

Soak corn in cold water for thirty minutes.

Preheat radiant oven to 400°.

Place corn on a small baking sheet, and roast until kernels are softened, approximately fifty minutes. Husk corn, and scrape kernels from cob. Measure 3 tablespoons of corn for crab filling; chop, and reserve. Pour remaining corn into a small saucepan, and stir in heavy cream. Place saucepan over a medium flame, and bring to a gentle boil. Adjust flame to low, and simmer until roasted corn cream begins to thicken stirring occasionally. Purée corn cream, pour into saucepan, cover and reserve.

Procedure for Crab-Stuffed Pillows:

Combine crab meat, reserved roasted corn, carrot, celery, parsley, lemon juice, and 1 tablespoon chives. Fold in heavy cream, season lightly and refrigerate.

Heat a seasoned crêpe pan over a medium-high flame. Brush pan lightly with *clarified butter* for the first crêpe only. Pour 1 3/4 ounce batter into the center of pan, tilting to evenly distribute. Cook briefly until edges are browned, flip with fingertips and cook for one minute. Slide crêpe onto work surface, and repeat procedure with remaining batter to equal eight crêpes.

Preheat radiant oven to 375°. Brush a 9-inch baking dish with *clarified butter*.

Place a heaping tablespoon of crab filling onto the center of one crêpe, tuck in edges, and fold to form a pillow shape. Repeat filling and forming remaining crêpes. Tuck crêpes snugly into prepared pan, and sprinkle with grated cheese. Bake until cheese is golden approximately fifteen minutes.

Heat roasted corn cream over a low flame, stirring frequently until warmed.

Plating:

Spoon a pool of roasted corn cream onto the center of four warmed square plates. Nestle two pillows overlapping onto sauce, and sprinkle with chives.

Yield:

four servings

brunoise: to cut to 1/8-inch square

clarified butter: To remove milk solids and water from butter: melt butter in a heavy saucepan over a low flame until milk solids fall to the bottom of the pan; discard foam from the surface, and pour butterfat into a small bowl leaving milk solids in bottom of pan. Discard solids.

Spinach Lasagna

Tomato Sauce

olive oil, as needed

2 medium Spanish onions, *small dice

4 cloves garlic, minced

freshly ground black pepper, as needed

2 tablespoons tomato paste

6 ounces freshly squeezed orange juice

2, 28-ounce cans quality plum tomatoes and juices, chopped

1 large bay leaf

salt and cayenne, sparingly to taste

Lasagna

tomato sauce (see Procedure)

1 pound dried lasagna noodles

salt, as needed

olive oil, as needed

1 large Spanish onion, *small dice

1/2 tablespoon garlic, minced

freshly ground black pepper, as needed

15 ounces leaf spinach, stemmed (weight after stemming)

2 pounds whole milk ricotta

3 ounces and 1/4 cup Parmigiano Reggiano, grated and divided

1/4 cup parsley, finely chopped, and additional to garnish

1 extra large egg, room temperature

1 extra large egg yolk, room temperature

1 pound and 1/4 cup mozzarella, shredded and divided

Procedure for Tomato Sauce:

Place a small stainless *rondeau* over a low flame, and film pan with olive oil. Add onions, garlic, and a generous grinding of black pepper, and *sweat*. Stir in tomato paste, and cook for five minutes.

Adjust flame to high, add orange juice, and stir constantly until syrupy. Add plum tomatoes and juices. Bring mixture to the boil, adjust flame to low; add bay leaf, and simmer sauce for one hour stirring occasionally. Season sauce sparingly, remove bay leaf, and reserve.

Procedure for Lasagna:

Three-fourths fill an eight quart pasta pot with cold water, and bring to the boil; salt the water to taste the salt. Cook noodles, drain, and rinse with cold water. Lay noodles in a single layer onto sheets of parchment. Cover noodles with another sheet of parchment to prevent drying.

Film an eight inch sauté pan with oil, and place over a low flame. Add onion, garlic, and a generous grinding of black pepper, and *sweat*. Scrape vegetables into a medium-sized stainless bowl.

Rinse, drain, and spin-dry spinach. Pour one inch of cold water into a small *rondeau*. Salt the water to taste the salt, and bring to the boil. Insert a vegetable steamer basket into *rondeau*, pack with spinach and cover. Steam spinach for two minutes; transfer spinach to a tea towel. Roll, and wring out moisture. Chop spinach.

Combine spinach, ricotta, 3 ounces Parmigiano Reggiano, and parsley with onion and garlic mixture, and season. Stir in egg and yolk.

Film a 9 x 13 x 2-inch baking pan with oil. Preheat radiant oven to 375°. Layer ingredients into prepared pan as follows:

sauce, thin layer

noodles, one layer overlapping

half of spinach-ricotta mixture

half pound mozzarella

repeat ingredients, using half of remaining sauce

noodles, one layer overlapping

remaining sauce

1/4 cup Parmigiano Reggiano, and 1/4 cup mozzarella, combined

Cover pan tightly with foil, and place on a baking sheet. Bake lasagna for fifty minutes. Remove foil, and continue to bake until sauce bubbles around edges and cheese is golden brown approximately twenty-five minutes.

Allow lasagna to rest for twenty minutes before serving.

Plating:

Cut lasagna into nine portions. Center lasagna on large plates, and garnish with parsley.

Yield:

nine servings

small dice: to cut to 1/4-inch square

rondeau: a shallow, wide, straight-sided pot with handles

sweat: to cook without color in a small amount of fat over a low flame

Apricot-Glazed Shrimp Cocktail

Apricot Marinade

12 ounces apricot nectar

1 tablespoon shallot, minced

1 teaspoon Grey Poupon® Dijon mustard

1 tablespoon fresh lime juice

2 ounces apple cider vinegar

freshly ground pepper, as needed

3 ounces olive oil

3 ounces canola oil

salt, as needed

Apricot Glazed Shrimp Cocktail

20, 16/20 raw shrimp, presplit, peeled, and cleaned

1/2 ounce red leaf lettuce, *chiffonade*

1/2 ounce arugula, *chiffonade*

1/2 apricot, pitted, *small dice*

1 ounce red onion, very thinly sliced

salt and freshly ground black pepper, as needed

canola oil, as needed

4 thin slices lime, twisted into an *S* shape, to garnish

Procedure for Apricot Marinade:

Pour apricot nectar into a small saucepan, and place over a medium flame. Slowly reduce nectar to approximately two ounces stirring occasionally. Pour into food processor work bowl fitted with steel blade. Allow nectar to cool to room temperature. Add shallot, Dijon, lime juice, and vinegar, season with black pepper and process to blend. Combine oils. With machine running, slowly add oil to emulsify; season lightly with salt. Pour three ounces into a lidded glass jar, cover, and reserve this marinade for tossing lettuce mix. Pour remaining marinade into a small lidded container, stir in shrimp, cover and refrigerate for two hours.

Procedure for Apricot Glazed Shrimp Cocktail:

Combine lettuce, arugula, apricot, and red onion in a small bowl; cover with a dampened tea towel and refrigerate.

Preheat grill over a medium-high flame.

Strain marinated shrimp through a sieve set over a small bowl. Transfer shrimp to a large plate, and season lightly. Use marinade for glazing.

Lightly dress lettuce mix with reserved marinade, season with black pepper and toss to coat. Divide mix between four stemmed wine glasses.

Lightly coat grate with oil. Stir marinade, generously glaze shrimp and grill.

Plating:

Arrange five shrimp onto the rim of each wine glass. Garnish cocktails with a lime twist.

Yield:

four servings

*chiffonade: to finely julienne

*small dice: to cut to 1/4-inch square

Penne with Shallot, Garlic, Roma Tomato, and Basil

8 ounces dried penne pasta

salt, as needed

4 1/4 ounces extra virgin olive oil

2 shallots, minced

2 large cloves garlic, minced

2 tablespoons tomato paste

freshly ground black pepper, as needed

dash cayenne

2 Roma tomatoes, *small dice*

4 tablespoons basil, *chiffonade*

Parmigiano Reggiano, as needed

Procedure:

Three-fourths fill a six quart pasta pot with cold water and bring to the boil; season with salt to taste the salt.

Heat oil in a small saucepan placed over a very low flame. Stir in shallots, garlic, tomato paste, season with black pepper and cayenne, and barely simmer for ten minutes. Add tomatoes, and remove from heat.

Cook penne al dente; drain, do not rinse. Pour back into pot, and stir in oil mixture. Adjust seasoning.

Plating:

Spoon pasta onto warmed square plates, and garnish with basil. Pass Parmigiano Reggiano and grater.

Yield:

four servings

small dice: to cut to 1/4-inch square

chiffonade: to finely julienne

ೲ

Pain Ordinare

8 ounces warm water, 105°
dash granulated sugar
1/4 ounce dry active yeast
13 ounces bread flour
1 1/2 teaspoon salt
olive oil, as needed
cornmeal, as needed
unbleached all purpose flour, as needed

Procedure:

Pour 8 ounces water into a warmed 5-quart KitchenAid® mixer bowl. Sprinkle water with sugar and yeast, and whisk to combine. Allow yeast to *proof* for ten minutes.

Attach dough hook to mixer, turn speed to Stir, and steadily add flour until dough begins to form. Add salt. Add additional flour or water as needed to achieve a slightly moist dough. Knead on speed 2 for seven minutes.

Turn dough out onto work surface and finish *kneading* by hand until dough feels smooth and elastic. Lightly oil a medium-sized bowl. Place dough into bowl, oiled side up. Cover bowl with plastic wrap and a tea towel. Allow dough to rise in a warm area until doubled in bulk.

Gently deflate dough with fist, re-cover, and rise until nearly doubled. Line a baking sheet with parchment, and dust with cornmeal.

Turn dough out onto work surface, and flatten. Cover with a dampened tea towel, and rest for five minutes. Re-flatten dough. Using a bench scraper push dough into the shape of a rectangle, and square the edges. Turn top edge down one-half inch, and form a tight seal. Roll dough into a log shape, and seal the final seam.

Scale dough into twelve portions. Gently form each portion into an oval shape. Use a bench scraper to lift each oval onto prepared baking sheet. Cover with a dampened tea towel, and rise until dough is puffy and doubled in bulk.

Preheat radiant oven to 400°. Fill a cake pan with water.

Lightly sift rolls with flour. Set cake pan on bottom shelf of oven, and place rolls on center rack. Firmly hit the cake pan so water splashes. Immediately close the oven door.

Bake rolls for fifteen minutes. Turn baking sheet, and continue to bake until golden brown approximately eight minutes. Cool completely on a rack.

Yield:

twelve rolls

proof: to allow yeast to rise

knead: to develop gluten in dough to expand and hold carbon dioxide

Miniature Corn Muffins

pan spray, as needed

2 cups unbleached all purpose flour

1 cup cornmeal

1/8 cup granulated sugar

3/4 tablespoon baking powder

1/2 teaspoon salt

1 large egg, lightly beaten, room temperature

8 ounces whole milk

2 ounces unsalted butter, melted and cooled

Procedure:

Pan spray seventeen 2-inch diameter muffin tins, and place on a baking sheet.

Preheat radiant oven to 375°.

Sift flour, cornmeal, sugar, baking powder, and salt into a medium-sized bowl.

Combine egg and milk in a small bowl; whisk in butter. Pour liquid over dry ingredients, and stir just until combined. Do *not* over mix.

Using a small cookie scoop (size 24) fill prepared tins three-fourths full with muffin mix.

Bake muffins for twelve minutes, turn baking sheet, and continue to bake until firm to the touch approximately three minutes.

Allow muffins to cool in tins for five minutes. Turn out of tins. Cool completely on a rack.

Yield:

seventeen muffins

Black Currant Dinner Rolls

7 ounces warm water, 105°

1/2 tablespoon honey

1/4 ounce dry active yeast

1 ounce unsalted butter, melted

12 ounces bread flour

1 1/2 teaspoon (heaping) salt

1/8 cup dried black currants, chopped

safflower oil, as needed

unbleached all purpose flour, as needed

Procedure:

Pour 7 ounces water and honey into a warmed 5-quart KitchenAid® mixer bowl, sprinkle in yeast, and whisk to combine. Let yeast *proof* for ten minutes. Stir in melted butter.

Attach dough hook to mixer, add flour and begin *kneading* on Stir speed until dough begins to form. Add salt. Add additional flour or water as needed to achieve a slightly moist soft dough. *Knead* on speed 2 for four minutes. Add currants, and continue to *knead* for two minutes.

Turn dough out onto work surface, and finish *kneading* by hand until dough feels smooth and elastic.

Lightly oil a medium-sized bowl. Place dough into bowl, oiled side up. Cover bowl with plastic wrap and a tea towel. Allow dough to rise in a warm area until doubled in bulk.

Line a baking sheet with parchment.

Turn dough out onto work surface, and flatten. Cover with a dampened tea towel, and rest for five minutes.

Roll to *2 fold* dough. Cover with dampened tea towel, and rest for five minutes.

Scale dough into one and three-quarter ounce portions. Using dampened hands gently *round*, and place on prepared baking sheet. Cover with dampened tea towel, and rise just until doubled in bulk.

Preheat radiant oven to 375°.

Dust rolls with flour, and cut one slash into tops.

Bake rolls for fifteen minutes, turn baking sheet, and continue to bake until golden brown approximately ten minutes.

Cool completely on a rack.

Yield:

thirteen rolls

proof: to allow yeast to rise

knead: to develop gluten in dough to expand and hold carbon dioxide

2 fold: Square flattened dough. Beginning at top of the dough, fold one-half down; gently seal seam. Bring bottom of dough up and over forming a log shape, and gently seal seam.

round: to shape dough into a tight, smooth ball

Cracked Wheat Rolls

Sponge

8 ounces warm water, 105°

1/2 ounce honey

1/4 ounce dry active yeast

1 1/2 ounce milk

1 ounce refined sunflower oil

1 cup whole wheat flour

Rolls

1 cup whole wheat flour

1 cup unbleached all purpose flour

dash dry active yeast

2 ounces warm water, 105°

1/2 cup white bulgur (cracked wheat berries)

1/2 tablespoon (heaping) salt

refined sunflower oil, as needed

cornmeal, as needed

1 1/2 ounce unsalted butter, melted and cooled

Procedure for Sponge:

Pour 8 ounces water and honey into a warmed 5-quart KitchenAid® mixer bowl; sprinkle in yeast, and whisk to dissolve. Stir in milk and oil, and combine well. Stir in 1 cup whole wheat flour just until smooth. Cover bowl with plastic wrap, and place in a warm area. Allow *sponge* to triple in bulk approximately two hours.

Procedure for Rolls:

Attach dough hook to mixer, add whole wheat and all purpose flours, dash yeast, 2 ounces warm water, and bulgur to *sponge*. *Knead* on Stir speed until dough begins to form. Add salt. Make all purpose flour adjustment as needed to achieve a moist sticky dough. *Knead* for seven minutes on speed 2.

Turn dough out onto a lightly floured work surface, and finish kneading by hand until dough feels smooth and elastic. Lightly oil a medium-sized bowl. Place dough into bowl, oiled side up. Cover bowl with plastic wrap and a tea towel. Allow dough to rise in a warm area until doubled in bulk.

Line a baking sheet with parchment, and dust with cornmeal. Turn dough out onto work surface, and flatten. Cover with a dampened tea towel, and rest for five minutes.

Roll to *2-fold* dough. Cover with dampened tea towel, and rest for five minutes.

Scale dough into two ounce portions. Using dampened hands gently *round*, and place on prepared baking sheet. Cover with dampened tea towel, and rise until doubled in bulk.

Preheat radiant oven to 400°. Brush rolls completely with melted butter, and cut one slash into tops.

Bake for fifteen minutes, turn baking sheet, and continue to bake until golden brown approximately ten minutes.

Cool completely on a rack.

Yield:

thirteen rolls

sponge: a thick yeast batter fermented to a spongy consistency

proof: to allow yeast to rise

knead: to develop gluten in dough to expand and hold carbon dioxide

2 fold: Square flattened dough. Beginning at top of the dough, fold one-half down; gently seal seam. Bring bottom of dough up and over forming a log shape, and gently seal seam.

round: to shape dough into a tight, smooth ball

ૐ

Corn Chowder

2 ears corn

1 1/2 cup Spanish onion, *small dice*, divided

1 1/2 cup carrot, *small dice*, divided

1 1/2 cup celery, *small dice*, divided

sachet d' èpices tied in cheesecloth (3 stems parsley, 1/2 teaspoon dried thyme, 1 clove garlic, peeled, 1 bay leaf, and 3 black peppercorns)

48 ounces cold water

1 ounce unsalted butter

2 cups waxy potatoes, peeled, *small dice* and divided

12 ounces light cream

1/2 cup lima beans, cooked

salt and white pepper, to taste

parsley, finely chopped, to garnish

Procedure:

Soak corn in cold water for thirty minutes.

Preheat radiant oven to 400°.

Place corn on a baking sheet, and roast until kernels are softened approximately fifty minutes. Husk both ears of corn; scrape kernels from one ear only, and reserve. Combine corn cob, roasted ear of corn, 1 cup onion, 1/2 cup carrot, 1/2 cup celery, *sachet d' épices*, and 48 ounces cold water in a small *rondeau*, and bring to the boil. Reduce flame to low, and simmer for forty-five minutes. Strain corn stock through a sieve into a medium-sized bowl. Press on solids to release juices; discard solids.

Melt butter in a medium-sized *rondeau* placed over a low flame. Add remaining onion, 1/2 cup each carrot and celery, and *sweat* vegetables. Stir in 1/2 cup potato and corn stock, and bring to the boil. Adjust flame to low, and simmer chowder base until potato is soft.

Pour cream into a small saucepan, and set over a low flame.

Strain chowder base through a sieve placed over a medium-sized bowl; reserve liquid and vegetables separately. Purée vegetables until smooth adding liquid as needed. Rinse *rondeau*, and pour in purée. Steadily whisk in liquid to fully incorporate. Stir in remaining carrots, celery, and potatoes, add cream, and bring chowder to the boil. Adjust flame to low, and simmer until potatoes are tender stirring occasionally. Add lima beans and reserved corn kernels, and heat through. Adjust seasoning to taste.

Plating:

Ladle chowder into large warmed bowls. Garnish with a pinch of parsley.

Yield:

four servings

small dice: to cut to 1/4-inch square

sachet d' épices: a small packet of aromatic spices

rondeau: a shallow, wide, straight-sided pot with handles

sweat: to cook without color in a small amount of fat over a low flame

Sorrel Vichyssoise

Crème Fraîche

1 cup heavy cream

1 tablespoon buttermilk, fresh and well-shaken

Vegetable Stock

1 ounce unsalted butter

1 medium Spanish onion, *medium dice*

2 medium carrots, *medium dice*

2 stalks celery, *medium dice*

2 ounces button mushroom stems, rinsed

sachet d' épices tied in cheesecloth (3 parsley stems, 1/2 teaspoon dried thyme,
1 clove garlic, peeled, 1 bay leaf, and 3 black peppercorns)

24 ounces cold water

Vichyssoise

12 ounces waxy potato, peeled and *medium dice* (weight after peeling)

salt, as needed

1 ounce unsalted butter

1/2 cup shallots, minced

1 teaspoon garlic, minced

6 ounces sorrel leaves, stemmed

lemon juice, freshly squeezed, to taste

white pepper and cayenne, to taste

chives, minced, to garnish

Procedure for Crème Fraîche:

Combine heavy cream and buttermilk by stirring in a clean glass jar with a lid. Place in a warm space in the kitchen, lidded and undisturbed, for thirty-six hours.

Refrigerate crème fraîche. It will continue to thicken and will remain fresh for one week. Lightly whisk to serve.

Procedure for Vegetable Stock:

Half fill a large stainless bowl with ice and water. Place a small soup pot over a low flame, add butter and melt. Stir in onion, carrots, celery, and mushroom stems; *sweat vegetables. Add *sachet d' épices and water, and bring to the boil. Adjust flame to low; simmer stock for forty-five minutes. Strain into a medium-sized stainless bowl. Press on vegetables to release juices; discard vegetables. Place bowl atop ice bath, undisturbed, until stock is cold. Remove, and discard congealed fat.

Procedure for Vichyssoise:

Pour potato into a two quart saucepan; cover with cold water, season to taste the salt, and bring to the boil. Cook potato until tender but not falling apart. Drain thoroughly through a small sieve.

Heat a ten inch stainless sauté pan over a low flame, add butter and melt. Add shallots and garlic; *sweat. Stir in sorrel, adjust flame to high, cover and cook for one minute. Scrape mixture into food processor work bowl inserted with metal blade; add potato and purée until smooth. Whip purée and 1/2 cup crème fraîche into cooled stock, and season to taste. Cover, and chill vichyssoise for four hours to develop flavor.

Plating:

Lightly whisk vichyssoise; adjust seasoning as needed. Pour into four glass cups. Garnish with chives, and serve on doily-lined saucers.

Yield:

four servings

*medium dice: to cut to 1/3-inch square

*sachet d' épices: a small packet of aromatic spices

*sweat: to cook without color in a small amount of fat over a low flame

*rondeau: a shallow, wide, straight-sided pot with handles

Gazpacho

1 pound ripened Roma tomatoes, seeded and *small dice*

4 ounces fresh corn kernels

1 poblano pepper, seeded and *small dice*

1 small jalapeño, seeded and minced

1 cucumber, peeled, seeded and *small dice*

5 scallions, white part only, sliced

2 ounces red onion, *small dice*

2 cloves garlic, minced

lime juice, freshly squeezed, as needed

16 ounces tomato juice

4 ounces cold water

salt and freshly ground black pepper, to taste

sugar and cayenne, sparingly to taste

scallion greens, very thinly sliced, to garnish

Procedure:

Combine tomatoes, corn, poblano, jalapeño, cucumber, scallions, red onion, and garlic in a medium-sized bowl.

Combine 2 ounces lime juice, tomato juice, and cold water, and season lightly. Combine seasoned liquid with vegetables. Cover bowl with plastic wrap, and refrigerate for several hours to allow flavors to develop. Taste, and adjust seasoning. Brighten flavor with lime juice as needed before serving.

Plating:

Ladle gazpacho into cold soup bowls, and scatter with scallion greens.

Yield:

six servings

small dice: to cut to 1/4-inch square

Fresh Tomato-Basil Cream

olive oil, as needed

1 large Spanish onion, *small dice*

1 carrot, *small dice*

1 stalk celery, *small dice*

1/2 tablespoon freshly ground black pepper

1 tablespoon garlic, minced

2 tablespoons tomato paste

2 tablespoons dried basil

4 ounces brandy

5 pounds ripened Beefsteak tomatoes, stemmed and *medium dice*

1 bay leaf

12 ounces heavy cream

salt and cayenne, to taste

basil, *chiffonade*, to garnish

Procedure:

Heat a medium-sized stainless *rondeau over a medium-low flame, and film with oil. Add onion, carrot, celery, black pepper, and garlic; *sweat vegetables. Stir in tomato paste, and cook for five minutes. Adjust flame to medium-high, add brandy and *flambé. When flames extinguish reduce until syrupy stirring constantly. Add tomatoes with juices and bay leaf. Bring to the boil, reduce flame to low, and simmer for one hour.

Pour cream into a one quart saucepan, and place over a medium flame. Reduce volume by half whisking occasionally.

Pass tomato mixture through a large-hole *chinois placed over a deep, tall pot. Press on mixture to extract juices; discard tomato mixture. Rinse *rondeau, and pour in tomato broth. Bring to a low boil over a medium flame. Whisk in reduced cream. Cook soup to consistency and depth of flavor whisking occasionally, and season to taste.

Plating:

Ladle tomato-basil cream into warmed bowls, and garnish with a pinch of basil.

Yield:

four servings

*small dice: to cut to 1/4-inch square

*medium dice: to cut to 1/3-inch square

*chiffonade: to finely julienne

*rondeau: a shallow, wide, straight-sided pot with handles

*sweat: to cook without color in a small amount of fat over a low flame

*flambé: to pour spirits over food and ignite

*chinois: a conical sieve

∽

Watercress Salad with Avocado and Shaved Asiago
~creamy garlic dressing

Dressing

1/2 ounce Asiago cheese, grated

1/2 teaspoon anchovy paste

2 medium cloves garlic, minced with a dash of salt

3/4 teaspoon freshly ground black pepper

1/3 cup mayonnaise

1/8 cup sour cream

2 ounces buttermilk

Salad

4 ounces watercress

3 ounces red leaf, torn bite-sized

1 avocado, ripened

2 ounces Asiago cheese

salt and freshly ground black pepper, to taste

Procedure for Dressing:

Combine Asiago, anchovy paste, garlic, and black pepper in a small bowl. Whisk in mayonnaise, sour cream, and buttermilk, and refrigerate.

Procedure for Salad:

Soak watercress in cold water to release dirt; lift out. Rinse and spin-dry greens. Combine in a medium-sized bowl, cover with a dampened tea towel, and refrigerate. Shave Asiago with the slicing edge of a box grater onto a plate.

Plating:

Season and dress greens, toss to coat, and mound on four chilled small plates. Peel, pit, and slice avocado into eight wedges; arrange two wedges on each plate. Pile shaved Asiago on top of dressed greens.

Yield:

four servings

Ratatouille Salad with Fresh Buffalo Mozzarella

1 small eggplant, sliced

salt, as needed

olive oil, as needed

1/2 small red onion, *medium dice*

1 small yellow pepper, *medium dice*

1 small green pepper, *medium dice*

2 cups button mushroom caps, cleaned and quartered

2 teaspoons garlic, minced

freshly ground black pepper, as needed

1 small zucchini, seeded and *medium dice*

1 ounce tomato purée

1 sprig basil

2 large Roma tomatoes, seeded and *medium dice*

4 ounces farm produced buffalo mozzarella, *small dice*

4 Bibb lettuce leaves

4 small basil bouquets, to garnish

Procedure:

Place eggplant into a colander, and season generously with salt. Set a heavy plate over eggplant for forty-five minutes. Thoroughly rinse eggplant, drain, and towel-dry. *Medium dice* eggplant.

Heat a ten inch sauté pan over a medium-high flame; film with oil. *Sauté* onion and peppers quickly so vegetables remain crisp. Transfer into a small bowl.

Add additional oil as needed to film pan. Briefly *sauté* mushrooms with garlic, season with black pepper, and stir constantly with a rubber spatula. Do *not* allow garlic to darken; add to onion and peppers.

Sauté eggplant and zucchini briefly. Stir in purée, basil sprig, and reserved vegetables with accumulated juices. Adjust flame to low, and simmer for five minutes to develop flavor. Add tomatoes, and season to taste.

Pour ratatouille onto a baking sheet; cool slightly. Refrigerate until cold.

Plating:

Remove basil sprig from ratatouille, and gently fold in mozzarella. Center lettuce leaves on four chilled small plates. Fill with ratatouille salad, and garnish with basil bouquet.

Yield:

four servings

medium dice: to cut to 1/3-inch square

small dice: to cut to 1/4-inch square

sauté: to cook quickly in a small amount of fat

Caesar Salad

Garlic Croutons

2 ounces olive oil

1 ounce salted butter

2 large cloves garlic, minced

1 shallot, minced

1 tablespoon parsley, chopped

1/2 tablespoon rosemary, chopped

dash cayenne

salt and freshly ground black pepper, to taste

4 ounces French bread, crusts removed, cut to 1 x 1/2-inch cubes

Caesar Dressing

2 large eggs, room temperature

2 medium cloves garlic, minced

1/2 tablespoon whole grain Grey Poupon® Dijon mustard

3/4 teaspoon anchovy paste

1 ounce fresh lemon juice

freshly ground black pepper, as needed

dash cayenne

1/4 cup Parmigiano Reggiano, grated

4 ounces extra virgin olive oil

4 ounces safflower oil

salt, scantly to taste

Salad

    1 1/2 heads Romaine lettuce, rinsed, spin-dried, and torn bite-sized

        salt, and freshly ground black pepper, to taste

        freshly grated Parmigiano Reggiano, to garnish

Procedure for Croutons:

    Pour olive oil into a small saucepan, add butter and heat over a very low flame until melted. Stir in garlic, shallot, parsley, rosemary, and cayenne; season with salt and black pepper, and barely simmer for ten minutes.

    Preheat radiant oven to 350°.

    Pour bread cubes into a medium-sized bowl. Strain oil mixture through a sieve over bread cubes; toss to combine. Pour in a single layer onto a baking sheet, and place into oven. Stir after ten minutes to ensure even browning. Continue to bake until golden.

    Cool completely. Pour garlic croutons into an airtight container.

Procedure for Caesar Dressing:

Fill a small stainless bowl with ice and water.

Fill a small saucepan with water, place over a medium flame, and bring to a simmer. Gently place eggs, and *coddle* for two minutes. Immediately *shock* eggs in ice bath.

Place one whole egg and one yolk into food processor work bowl fitted with metal blade; discard remaining egg white. Add garlic, Dijon, and anchovy paste, and process to combine. Add lemon juice, a generous twist of black pepper, cayenne, and Parmigiano Reggiano, and process thoroughly. Combine oils. With machine running, slowly add oil to emulsify. Adjust seasoning as necessary. Pour dressing into a lidded container, cover, and refrigerate.

Procedure for Salad:

Place romaine into a large stainless bowl. Cover with a dampened tea towel, and refrigerate.

Plating:

Season romaine, dress generously, and toss to coat. Add garlic croutons, and toss lightly. Mound salad into deep bowls, and garnish with freshly grated Parmigiano Reggiano.

Yield:

four servings

coddle: to cook in water just below the boiling point

shock: to stop the cooking process

Chopped Salad with Spicy Chicken
~bacon ranch dressing

Bacon-Ranch Dressing

4 slices cob-smoked bacon

2 tablespoons red onion, minced

1 teaspoon garlic, minced

3/4 teaspoon freshly ground black pepper, and salt to taste

1/2 teaspoon New Mexico red chile powder

3/4 cup mayonnaise

1/4 cup sour cream

1/2 tablespoon fresh lime juice

3 ounces buttermilk

Salad

10 ounces buttermilk

12 ounces chicken tenders

4 slices cob-smoked bacon

8 ounces Roma tomatoes, *small dice*

6 ounces cucumber, peeled, seeded and *small dice*

6 ounces black olives, quartered

1/2 head romaine lettuce, rinsed, spin-dried, and chopped

1/2 head iceberg lettuce, rinsed, spin-dried, and chopped

3 ounces red onion, thinly sliced

salt and freshly ground black pepper, as needed

4 1/2 ounces unbleached all purpose flour

3 teaspoons New Mexico red chile powder

3/4 teaspoon *each* sweet Hungarian paprika and cayenne

1/3 teaspoon *each* ground thyme, rubbed sage, and Bell's® seasoning

refined sunflower oil, as needed

Procedure for Bacon-Ranch Dressing:

Place bacon from both dressing and salad ingredients into a cold skillet. Cook over a low flame until crisp; drain on a paper towel-lined plate. Discard fat, wipe skillet with paper toweling, and place on stove top. Finely chop 4 slices of bacon, rough chop 4 slices, and reserve both separately.

Add red onion, garlic, black pepper, and red chile into a small bowl. Whisk in mayonnaise, sour cream, lime juice, and 3 ounces buttermilk. Stir in finely chopped bacon, and season lightly with salt. Pour dressing into a lidded jar, cover, and refrigerate.

Procedure for Salad:

Pour 10 ounces buttermilk into a lidded container; fully immerse chicken, cover, and refrigerate for two hours.

Separately place tomatoes, cucumber, and black olives into small bowls, cover with plastic wrap, and refrigerate. Combine lettuces and red onion in a large bowl; cover with a dampened tea towel, and refrigerate.

Transfer chicken onto a rack-lined baking sheet. Remove excess moisture with paper toweling, and season with salt and black pepper. Combine flour and spices in a zipped bag. Drop a few pieces of chicken into bag, shake to fully coat, and return to rack. Continue procedure with remaining chicken. Discard unused flour. Preheat radiant oven to 200°.

Heat a ten inch skillet over a medium flame, add 1/2-inch oil and thoroughly heat. *Pan-fry* chicken in batches until evenly golden brown and fully cooked. Transfer onto a small baking sheet, and hold in warm oven.

Plating:

Season lettuce mix, dress generously, and toss to coat. Add chopped bacon, and toss. Pile salad high on four large plates. Mound vegetables equal distance around salad. Arrange warm spicy chicken on top.

Yield:

four servings

small dice: to cut into 1/4-inch square

pan-fry: to cook coated food in a skillet of hot oil over a medium flame

ৎ

Roast Pork Loin with Rhubarb Sauce
~glazed yellow and green beans

2 3/4 pounds boneless pork loin, cleaned and trimmed

1 clove garlic, halved

dried thyme, as needed

sweet Hungarian paprika, as needed

freshly ground pepper, as needed

olive oil, as needed

salt, as needed

1 1/2 cup fresh rhubarb, chopped

1 1/2 ounce granulated sugar

1/2 pound yellow wax beans

1/2 pound green beans

2 1/2 ounces unsalted butter, cold and divided

3 tablespoons shallots, minced

1 teaspoon garlic, minced

2 ounces dry white wine

16 ounces **Chicken Stock** (see recipe for **Chicken Stock**, page 35)

1/2 teaspoon arrowroot combined with 1 teaspoon cold water for *slurry*

1 small bay leaf

2 ounces port wine

Procedure for Roast Pork Loin:

Rub loin with cut garlic and season generously with thyme, paprika, and black pepper. Rub lightly with oil. Allow loin to stand at room temperature for thirty minutes. Preheat radiant oven to 325°. Heat a ten inch cast-iron skillet over a medium-high flame. Season loin with salt, and *sear* evenly until golden. Roast loin to an internal temperature of 138°–140°.

Procedure for Glazed Beans and Rhubarb Sauce:

Combine rhubarb and sugar in a small bowl, and cover with plastic wrap. Allow fruit to soften at room temperature for thirty minutes stirring occasionally.

Pour approximately two inches of cold water into a three quart saucepan, and season with salt. Half fill a medium-sized bowl with ice and water. Snap off ends of beans, and remove any tough strings. Arrange yellow beans loosely in a steamer basket. Bring seasoned water fully to the boil, insert basket and cover. Steam until beans are tender yet crisp to the bite. Immediately *shock* in ice bath. Repeat procedure with green beans. Drain beans thoroughly, combine and refrigerate.

Transfer roast pork to a baking sheet, and tent lightly with foil. Place the skillet over a low-medium flame, add 1/2 ounce butter and melt. Stir in shallots and garlic, season with black pepper, and briefly *sweat*. Adjust flame to high, stir in white wine, and reduce until syrupy stirring constantly. Stir *slurry*. Immediately whisk in stock, *slurry*, bay leaf, and accumulated pork juices. Skim and discard impurities from surface, and reduce to a thin sauce consistency. Adjust flame to medium, stir in rhubarb and port, and cook to develop depth of flavor stirring occasionally. Remove from heat. Whisk in 1 ounce butter, remove bay leaf, and adjust seasoning.

Pour 2 ounces water and remaining butter into a ten inch sauté pan, and bring to the boil. Add beans, season lightly, and toss until liquid evaporates and beans are evenly glazed and hot.

Transfer loin to a cutting board. Slice diagonally into twelve slices.

Plating:

Place three slices of pork loin overlapping on four large warmed plates. Ladle generously with sauce, and arrange plates with beans.

Yield:

four servings

*slurry: a starch and cool liquid paste, cooked and used as a thickener

*sear: to brown the surface of food in fat over a high flame

*shock: to stop the cooking process

*sweat: to cook without color in a small amount of fat over a low flame

Tequila-Lime Swordfish with Roasted Corn and Poblano Salsa
~parsley red potatoes

Tequila-Lime Marinade

4 ounces tequila

3 ounces fresh lime juice

1 1/2 teaspoon garlic, minced

1 1/2 teaspoon honey

1 teaspoon New Mexico red chile powder

canola oil, as needed

4, 6-ounce U.S. harpoon swordfish steaks

salt and white pepper, as needed

Roasted Corn and Poblano Salsa

2 ears corn

1 poblano pepper

olive oil, as needed

2 tablespoons Roma tomato, *small dice*

1 tablespoon cilantro, roughly chopped

2 tablespoons white onion, *small dice*

1/2 teaspoon garlic, minced

1 ounce fresh lime juice

freshly ground black pepper, to taste

Parsley Red Potatoes

1 pound red potatoes, 1 to 1 1/2-inch diameter

salt, as needed

1 ounce unsalted butter

1/4 teaspoon New Mexico red chile powder

freshly ground black pepper, to taste

parsley, finely chopped

Procedure for Marinating Swordfish:

Combine tequila, lime juice, garlic, honey, and chile powder in a small bowl; whisk in 2 ounces oil to emulsify.

Place swordfish into a shallow lidded container; pour marinade over fish, cover, and refrigerate for two hours.

Procedure for Roasted Corn and Poblano Salsa:

Soak corn in cold water for thirty minutes. Preheat radiant oven to 400°.

Place corn on a baking sheet. Rub poblano lightly with oil, and place in a small pan. Roast corn until kernels are softened approximately fifty minutes. Roast poblano until skin is lightly charred turning frequently. Place poblano into a small bowl, cover with plastic wrap, and steam for thirty minutes. Skin and seed poblano without rinsing, and *small dice*. Husk corn, and scrape kernels from cob. Combine corn kernels, poblano, tomato, cilantro, onion, garlic, and lime juice; season salsa lightly with black pepper.

Preheat grill over a high flame. Remove swordfish from marinade, and season with salt and white pepper; reserve marinade.

Procedure for Parsley Red Potatoes and Grilling Swordfish:

Rinse potatoes, and cut in half. Pour into a four and a half quart saucepan, and cover with cold water; salt the water to taste the salt, and bring to the boil. Cook potatoes until a paring knife slides through easily approximately five to seven minutes.

Lightly coat grate with oil. Brush swordfish with marinade, and grill to preferred degree of doneness.

Drain potatoes. Melt butter in a ten inch sauté pan, add potatoes, and roll to coat evenly; season with chile powder, salt, and black pepper.

Plating:

Center swordfish on warmed large plates, and generously mound with salsa. Encircle fish with potatoes, and sprinkle with parsley.

Yield:

four servings

small dice: to cut to 1/4-inch square

Teriyaki-Marinated Tri-Tip Sirloin
~parmesan and gruyère whipped potatoes

Teriyaki Marinade

8 ounces **Veal Stock** (see recipe for **Veal Stock**, page 49)

2 ounces teriyaki sauce

1 ounce Worcestershire sauce

2 ounces red wine vinegar

2 ounces fresh lemon juice

1 1/2 tablespoon Coleman's® dry mustard

1 small clove garlic, minced

1 tablespoon ginger, grated

parsley, finely chopped as needed

1 teaspoon freshly ground black pepper

1 1/2 pound beef *tri-tip sirloin*

canola oil, as needed

salt, as needed

Parmesan and Gruyère Whipped Potatoes

2 1/2 pounds waxy potatoes, peeled and *large dice* (weight after peeling)

salt, as needed

12 ounces heavy cream

5 ounces unsalted butter

2 1/2 ounces Parmigiano Reggiano, grated

2 1/2 ounces Gruyère, grated

white pepper, to taste

Procedure for Marinating Tri-Tip Sirloin:

Pour stock, teriyaki sauce, Worcestershire sauce, red wine vinegar, lemon juice, dry mustard, garlic, ginger, 1 tablespoon parsley, and pepper into a small bowl, and whisk to combine. Place tri-tip into a shallow container. Pour teriyaki marinade evenly over beef, cover, and refrigerate. Marinate overnight.

Procedure for Parmesan and Gruyère Whipped Potatoes and Grilling Tri-Tip:

Preheat grill over a high flame.

Pour potatoes into a six quart pot, and cover with cold water by two inches. Salt the water to taste the salt, and bring to the boil. Cook potatoes until tender yet not falling apart. Pour heavy cream into a small saucepan, add butter, and heat over a medium-low flame until butter melts. Drain potatoes thoroughly. Pour into a 5-quart KitchenAid® mixer bowl, and attach flat beater. Beat potatoes on speed 2 until smooth. Replace flat beater with whip, add cheeses, and turn to speed 2. Steadily add hot cream and butter while increasing speed; whip until fluffy, season, and whip briefly. Scrape whipped potatoes into a microwaveable container, and cover loosely.

Lightly coat grate with oil. Season tri-tip with salt, and grill to preferred degree of doneness. Transfer to a cutting board.

Microwave potatoes for two minutes, and fold to evenly distribute heat. Microwave another two minutes.

Strain marinade into a small saucepan, place over a high flame, and bring to a full boil. Remove jus from heat. Thinly slice beef across the grain.

Plating:

Mound potatoes in the center of four large warmed plates, drape with five slices of beef slightly overlapping and fanned out. Ladle an ounce of jus over beef. Sprinkle with parsley.

Yield:

four servings

tri-tip sirloin: triangular shaped cut from the bottom of beef sirloin butt

large dice: to cut to 3/4-inch square

Fillet of Sole with Fines Herbs à la Meunière
~tarragon carrots

Tarragon Carrots

1 pound carrots, peeled and *batonnet*

1/2 teaspoon granulated sugar

1 ounce unsalted butter

1 1/2 tablespoon tarragon, finely chopped

Fillet of Sole with Fines Herbs à la Meunière

1 ounce *clarified butter*, divided

1 ounce refined sunflower oil, divided

4, 4-ounce Atlantic sole fillets

3 tablespoons fresh lemon juice, divided

salt and white pepper, as needed

3 ounces unbleached all purpose flour

2 large eggs, lightly beaten

1 teaspoon *each*: tarragon, parsley, chervil, and chives, finely chopped

2 ounces unsalted butter

Procedure for Tarragon Carrots:

Pour approximately two inches of cold water into a two quart saucepan, and season with 1/2 teaspoon sugar. Half fill a medium-sized stainless bowl with ice and water.

Arrange carrots loosely in a steamer basket. Bring seasoned water fully to the boil, insert basket, and cover. Steam carrots until tender yet crisp to the bite. Immediately *shock* in ice bath. Drain carrots, and refrigerate.

Add butter and 2 ounces water into a ten inch sauté pan, and set aside.

Procedure for Fillet of Sole with Fines Herbs à la Meunière:

Preheat radiant oven to 400°. If available, preheat another oven to 150°.

Divide *clarified butter* and sunflower oil equally between two ten inch Teflon® skillets, and heat thoroughly over a medium flame.

Season fillets with 1 teaspoon lemon juice, salt, and white pepper. Lightly dredge in flour; shake off excess. Dip in egg; allow excess to drip off. Place into skillets, and *pan-fry* until bottom sides are golden brown, turn fillets, and place pans into oven for eight minutes. Discard unused breading.

Place four large plates into warm oven.

Combine herbs.

Bring pan of butter and water to the boil; add carrots and tarragon, and toss until evenly glazed and hot. Turn off flame.

Heat 2 ounces butter in a small saucepan over a medium flame until foam subsides and butter is light brown. Remove saucepan from heat, and immediately plate entrée.

Plating:

Lift cooked fillets onto large warmed plates; sprinkle with herbs and remaining lemon juice. Scatter tarragon carrots at the top of plates. Pour hot browned butter over fillets creating a froth, and serve.

Yield:

four servings

batonnet: a long and rectangular cut, 1/4 x 1/4 x 2-inch

clarified butter: To remove milk solids and water from butter: melt butter in a heavy saucepan over a low flame until milk solids fall to the bottom of the pan; discard foam from the surface, and pour butterfat into a small bowl leaving milk solids in bottom of pan. Discard solids.

shock: to stop the cooking process

pan-fry: to cook coated food in a skillet of hot oil over a medium flame

&

Ganache Chocolate Mousse Cake
~chantilly cream

Soufflé Cake

9 ounces Callebaut® semisweet chocolate, chopped

1 1/2 ounce Callebaut® bittersweet chocolate, chopped

10 large egg yolks, room temperature

1 1/8 cup granulated sugar, divided

1 1/2 ounce brewed strong coffee, hot

3/4 teaspoon vanilla extract

1/4 teaspoon and 1/8 teaspoon salt, divided

11 large egg whites, room temperature

1 1/4 teaspoon (heaping) cream of tartar

Mousse

1 pound Callebaut® semisweet chocolate, chopped

12 ounces unsalted butter, *medium dice* and softened

8 large egg yolks, room temperature

12 large egg whites, room temperature

dash salt

1 1/2 teaspoon cream of tartar

80 grams granulated sugar

Ganache

1 pound Callebaut® semi sweet chocolate, finely chopped

14 ounces heavy cream

Chantily Cream, to garnish (recipe follows **Mousse Cake**)

Procedure for Soufflé Cake:

Preheat radiant oven to 350°.Line a half baking sheet pan with parchment.

Half fill a medium-sized *rondeau* with water. Place over a low flame, and bring to a simmer. Pour semisweet and bitter chocolate into a flat-bottomed medium-sized stainless bowl, and place over simmering water stirring occasionally until melted.

Half fill another medium-sized *rondeau* with water, place over a low flame, and bring to a simmer. Pour yolks and 1/2 cup sugar into a medium-sized stainless bowl, and place over simmering water; whisk until yolks have warmed. Pour yolk mixture into a 5-quart KitchenAid® mixer bowl, and whip until nearly tripled in volume, and pale yellow. Wash stainless bowl, and scrape yolk mixture into bowl.

Stir coffee, vanilla, and 1/4 teaspoon salt into melted chocolate. Thoroughly fold chocolate mixture into yolk mixture.

Pour egg whites into a 5-quart KitchenAid® mixer bowl, add 1/8 teaspoon salt and cream of tartar, and attach whip. Turn mixer speed to 4, and whip whites until foamy. Steadily add remaining sugar while increasing speed; whip to a satiny firm meringue—mixture should peak, and gently fall back when whip is lifted.

Fold one-fourth of meringue into chocolate mixture using a large balloon whisk. Fold remaining meringue into chocolate gently and thoroughly in three applications.

Pour onto prepared baking sheet smoothing gently to even batter. Bake until cake forms a thin crust, and yields softly to the touch approximately thirty minutes. Do *not* over bake.

Place cake on a rack to cool completely in pan. Guide a thin paring knife between cake and baking sheet to loosen cake. Place a sheet of parchment onto cake, cover with a half baking sheet flat side down, invert pans, and carefully peel off parchment. Cut out one 9-inch round, and cover with a tea towel. Freeze remaining soufflé cake for another use.

Procedure for Mousse:

Reheat water in *rondeau* to a simmer, add additional water as needed to reach half full. Pour chocolate into a flat-bottomed medium-sized stainless bowl, and place over simmering water stirring occasionally until melted. Whisk in softened butter, a little at a time, fully incorporating each addition. Whisk in yolks, two at a time, fully incorporating each addition. Remove bowl from heat. Cool mixture to 90°.

Pour whites into a 5-quart KitchenAid® mixer bowl, add salt and cream of tartar, and attach whip. Turn mixer speed to 4, and whip whites until foamy. Steadily add sugar while increasing speed, and whip to a soft meringue. Fold one-fourth of meringue into chocolate mixture using a balloon whisk. Fold remaining meringue into chocolate gently and thoroughly in three applications. Pour mousse into a 9-inch springform pan. Place soufflé cake round on top, and wrap pan tightly with plastic wrap. Freeze overnight.

Procedure for Ganache:

Pour chocolate into a medium-sized stainless bowl. Pour cream into a one quart saucepan, and bring to the boil. Immediately pour cream over chocolate to melt undisturbed for one minute. Gently stir cream into chocolate with a whisk until evenly combined and shiny. Allow ganache to cool for five minutes.

Place mousse cake, soufflé cake side down, on a 9-inch cake circle. Release and remove sides of pan, and carefully lift off bottom. Place cake on a small cooling rack, and set onto a baking sheet. Pour all of ganache onto center of cake. Tilt the rack to evenly distribute ganache. Do *not* use a spatula. Refrigerate cake on baking sheet for two hours. Transfer cake onto a flat serving plate using a 10 x 10-inch spatula. Scrape remaining ganache into a lidded container, cover, and refrigerate or freeze for another use.

Plating:

Slice mousse cake with a hot, dry slicing knife. Center slice on colorful plate. Pipe chantilly cream decoratively to garnish.

Yield:

sixteen servings

medium dice: to cut to 1/3-inch square

rondeau: a shallow, wide, straight-sided pot with handles

Chantilly Cream

8 ounces heavy cream, cold

3/4 tablespoon granulated sugar

1/2 teaspoon vanilla extract

Procedure:

Place 5-quart KitchenAid® mixer bowl and whip into refrigerator to chill until very cold.

Pour cream into cold bowl, and whip on medium speed until cream begins to hold shape. Add sugar and vanilla extract, and continue to whip until nearly firm peak. Do *not* over whip.

Cover with plastic wrap, and refrigerate. Gently whisk chantilly before use.

Yield:

one pint

Fresh Plum Tartlets
~black pepper scented ice cream

Hazelnut Pâte Sucrée

3/4 cup hazelnuts

6 3/4 ounces unbleached all purpose flour

2 3/4 ounces granulated sugar

dash salt

1 medium egg, lightly beaten

4 ounces unsalted butter, cold, and additional for tartlet pans

pastry flour, as needed

1 egg combined with 1 tablespoon cold water for egg wash

Streusel

1 1/3 ounce unsalted butter, softened

3 ounces light brown sugar

3 ounces granulated sugar

1/2 cup unbleached all purpose flour

1 1/4 teaspoon lemon zest, minced

1/4 teaspoon (scant) cinnamon

1/4 teaspoon (scant) nutmeg, freshly grated

1/4 cup hazelnuts

Fresh Plum Tartlets

1/3 cup granulated sugar

5 1/4 teaspoons Minute® Tapioca

1 tablespoon and 1/2 teaspoon fresh lemon juice

1/4 teaspoon (scant) cinnamon

dash salt

3 1/2 cups fresh purple plums, pitted and sliced

Black Pepper Scented Ice Cream (recipe follows **Plum Tartlets**)

Procedure for Hazelnut Pâte Sucrée:

Preheat radiant oven to 350°. Pour 3/4 cup and 1/4 cup hazelnuts onto a parchment-lined baking sheet. Bake nuts until lightly golden brown approximately ten minutes. Pour onto a thin towel, and rub vigorously to remove skins. Finely chop nuts; reserve 1/4 cup for streusel. Turn off oven.

Pour flour, sugar, and salt into food processor work bowl fitted with metal blade, and pulse on and off to combine. *Medium dice* butter, and scatter over flour mixture. Pulse on and off until mixture resembles coarse cornmeal. Add 3/4 cup finely chopped hazelnuts and egg; briefly pulse to combine.

Scrape dough onto a sheet of plastic wrap. Using edges of plastic gather dough. Fold plastic over dough, flatten to a disc, and place inside of a plastic bag. Refrigerate dough for three hours.

Butter four 4 1/2-inch tartlet pans.

Place unwrapped dough on a pastry-floured sheet of parchment. Dust dough with pastry flour, and cover with another sheet of parchment. Allow dough to slightly soften. Roll between parchment sheets to 1/8-inch thickness. Cut out four 5 1/2-inch rounds and gently form into prepared pans, reinforce sides.

Transfer tartlet shells to a baking sheet, and refrigerate for one hour. Wrap left-over dough in a sheet of plastic wrap, flatten, and freeze for another use.

Procedure for Streusel:

Place butter and both sugars into a medium-sized bowl. Cut in butter with a pastry blender just until combined.

Combine flour, zest, spices, and reserved 1/4 cup hazelnuts in a small bowl. Lightly toss into creamed mixture until nearly combined. Mixture will be uneven.

Procedure for Fresh Plum Tartlets:

Preheat radiant oven to 350°.

Prick bottoms and sides of shells with a fork. Line each shell with a 6-inch circle of waxed paper, and fill with beans.

Bake shells until sides begin to color approximately twelve minutes. Remove waxed paper and beans, lightly brush shells with egg wash, and continue to bake until bottoms appear dry approximately five minutes.

Cool tartlet shells on a rack. Adjust oven temperature to 375°.

Combine sugar, tapioca, lemon juice, cinnamon, and salt in a medium-sized stainless bowl; fold in plums.

Place shells on a baking sheet; mound with filling. Bake for twenty-five minutes. Place baking sheet on stove top. Sprinkle streusel onto tartlets, and gently press to adhere. Bake tartlets until filling begins to bubble and streusel is lightly golden brown approximately fifteen to twenty minutes.

Cool on a rack for thirty minutes. Carefully remove tartlet rims. Allow tartlets to cool completely. Remove bottom discs.

Plating:

Center tartlets on dessert plates, and garnish with a scoop of black pepper scented ice cream.

Yield:

four tartlets

medium dice: to cut to 1/3-inch square

Black Pepper-Scented Ice Cream

1/4 teaspoon finely ground black pepper

375 milliliters whole milk

125 milliliters heavy cream

125 grams granulated sugar, divided

6 large egg yolks, room temperature

Procedure:

Pour black pepper onto a small plate. Allow pepper to air uncovered overnight.

Place a two quart glass measure cup into a large stainless bowl, and pack bowl with ice. Set a fine sieve on top.

Pour milk, cream, and 60 grams sugar into a two quart saucepan; add pepper, and stir to combine. Bring mixture to the boil stirring frequently, cover, and remove from heat. Allow milk mixture to steep for ten minutes.

Pour yolks into a medium-sized bowl, and whisk in remaining sugar until thickened and pale yellow.

Uncover saucepan; bring mixture to the boil stirring frequently. Steadily whisk milk mixture into yolks to *temper*. Pour into saucepan, and place over a low flame. Stir custard cream constantly with a rubber spatula until it begins to thicken, and reaches 160°. Do *not* boil.

Immediately pass through sieve into glass measure cup. Pour cold water over ice to speed the cooling process. Stir custard cream frequently until cool approximately thirty minutes.

Pour into ice cream freezer, and proceed with manufacturer's directions.

Yield:

800 milliliters

temper: to incorporate a hot liquid into an egg mixture to equalize temperature

Raspberry and Grand Marnier Soufflé Glacé
~fresh raspberry sauce

Fresh Raspberry Sauce

340 grams fresh raspberries

85 grams granulated sugar

Raspberry and Grand Marnier Soufflé Glacé

700 milliliters heavy cream

1 teaspoon vanilla extract

distilled white vinegar, as needed

salt, as needed

220 grams granulated sugar

6 large egg yolks

30 milliliters Grand Marnier® liqueur

100 milliliters **Fresh Raspberry Sauce** (see Procedure)

fresh raspberries, to garnish

Procedure for Fresh Raspberry Sauce:

Combine berries and sugar in a medium-sized stainless bowl. Allow berries to soften until sugar is melted approximately forty-five minutes stirring occasionally. Pour berries into food processor work bowl fitted with metal blade, and purée until combined. Pass purée through a fine sieve into a small bowl. Press on seeds to extract juices; discard seeds. Stir sauce to combine. Measure 100 milliliters for soufflé glacé, and reserve. Pour remainder into a squeeze bottle.

Procedure for Raspberry and Grand Marnier Soufflé Glacé:

Refrigerate a 5-quart KitchenAid® mixer bowl and whip to chill. Line a collapsible terrine mold with plastic wrap, and smooth out creases.

Pour heavy cream into cold mixer bowl, and whip until it begins to hold shape. Add vanilla extract, and continue to whip to soft peak. Cover bowl with plastic wrap, and refrigerate.

Clean a copper sugar pot with vinegar and salt; thoroughly rinse. Pour sugar into pot, and cook over a medium flame to 275° soft crack—slow, big, open bubbles in center of pot.

Pour yolks into a 5-quart KitchenAid® mixer bowl. Whip on speed 2 while sugar is cooking. Quickly and steadily pour cooked sugar into yolks. Use a rubber spatula to scrape cooked sugar from the bottom of the pot. Increase speed to 4, and whip until bottom of mixer bowl is cool. Gently and thoroughly fold whipped cream into yolk mixture. Divide between two bowls. Fold reserved fresh raspberry sauce into one bowl, and Grand Marnier® into the other. Pour raspberry mixture evenly into terrine mold, and freeze for fifteen minutes. Pour in Grand Marnier layer, and smooth surface. Wrap terrine with plastic wrap, and freeze overnight.

Invert soufflé glacé onto a parchment-lined baking sheet. Release and remove mold, peel off plastic, and place into freezer. Use within thirty minutes, or wrap baking sheet tightly with plastic.

Plating:

Slice soufflé glacé into eight slices. Paint cold glass plates with raspberry sauce. Arrange each slice on plate, and decorate with fresh raspberries.

Yield:

eight servings

White Chocolate Timbales
~bing cherry sauce

grape seed oil, as needed

200 grams Callebaut® white chocolate, chopped

110 grams eggs, lightly beaten

1/2 teaspoon vanilla extract

200 milliliters whole milk

20 grams granulated sugar

Bing Cherry Sauce (recipe follows **White Chocolate Timbale**)

Chantilly Cream (see recipe for **Chantilly Cream**, page 122)

fresh Bing cherries, to garnish

Procedure:

Preheat radiant oven to 340°, and place oven rack in third lowest position.

Line a very small deep roasting pan with a layer of paper towels. Brush four 6-ounce timbale molds very lightly with oil. Place molds into roasting pan. Fill a kettle with water, and bring to the boil.

Half fill a small *rondeau* with water, and place over a low flame. Pour chocolate into a flat bottomed medium-sized stainless bowl. Place bowl over barely simmering water until completely melted. Stir to combine. Remove bowl from heat. Cool chocolate slightly.

Combine egg and vanilla extract. Steadily pour into warm chocolate while stirring to combine thoroughly. Mixture will appear curdled at first but will blend. Combine milk and sugar. Steadily pour into chocolate mixture while stirring to combine.

Pass mixture through a fine sieve into a one quart glass measure cup. Pour mixture into prepared molds. Pour boiled water into roasting pan to reach halfway up the sides of molds.

Bake timbales until firm approximately thirty to thirty-five minutes.

Remove timbales from pan to a rack. Cool to room temperature, cover with plastic wrap, and refrigerate overnight.

Plating:

Gently pull timbale from edge of mold with fingertips to release. Invert timbale onto the center of a rimmed dessert plate, and tap bottom of mold for full release. Ladle with Bing cherry sauce. Garnish with chantilly cream and fresh Bing cherries.

Yield:

four timbales

rondeau: a shallow, wide, straight-sided pot with handles

Bing Cherry Sauce

2 cups Bing cherries, pitted and quartered

3 ounces granulated sugar

2 teaspoons cold water

1/2 lemon, juiced

1/4 teaspoon vanilla extract

Procedure:

Pour cherries, sugar, and water into a small saucepan, and stir to combine. Bring mixture to a rolling boil. Pass through a sieve placed over a small bowl. Pour juices into saucepan, and pour cherries into bowl.

Place saucepan over a medium-low flame, stir in lemon juice, and simmer until juices thicken. Stir in cherries, increase flame to high, and bring to the boil. Boil sauce briefly until juices begin to re-thicken. Remove from heat. Stir in vanilla extract.

Allow sauce to cool to room temperature. Pour into a lidded container, cover, and refrigerate sauce until cold.

Yield:

eight ounces

The Autumn Season

An early morning walk reveals a sudden chill. Newly fallen snow dusts the Jay mountain range. Tall grasses are tipped with frost. Mist hangs suspended above the valley floor. The piercing honk of migrating Canadian geese slices the serenity of silence. A small unnamed pond is mirror still. As sunrise bathes Jay Peak, its image appears mirrored on the pond: a silhouette of soft ridges painted with autumn's palette of red, yellow, orange, purple, and gold.

Native Americans introduced squash to the early settlers. Winter squash has thickened skin and is a keeper if stored in a cool and airy place. Autumn's harvest yields buttercup, butternut, acorn, delicata, spaghetti, Hubbard, and pumpkin squashes. The superb aroma and meaty texture of freshly foraged mushrooms perfume delicate sauces and hearty stews. Holiday tables are graced with potatoes, onions, leeks, parsnips, carrots, beets, spinach, bell peppers, eggplant, cabbage, broccoli, cauliflower, fennel, winter chicories, cranberries, grapes, pears, apples, cider, black walnuts, beechnuts, imported chestnuts, and California pomegranates. Open season for hunting wild game begins in September, and carries through early winter. The earthy, deeply satisfying flavor of wild game is also available from game producers throughout Vermont.

A cozy wood fire illuminates the table set for two.

Venison Loin Roast with Sun Dried Cherry Sauce

Delicious, tender, and delicately flavored farm-raised venison and the fresh-picked-cherry aroma of Pinot Noir mingle with the perfume of piquant chile, black pepper, and sun-sweetened dried cherries. Caramelized sweet potato hash laced with rich and nutty-flavored browned butter accompanies this dish.

Hubbard Squash and Crystallized Ginger Tart

Mild, sweet, orange fleshed and dry textured Hubbard squash spiced with the warm, slightly sweet aromatic flavor of cinnamon, nutmeg, cloves, and ginger is blended into a silky custard, and baked to firm-textured smoothness in buttery-rich pastry. Luscious whipped cream sweetened with Meyer's rum, and peppered with the sharp flavor of crystallized ginger garnishes this tantalizing tart.

Inspiring.

ൟ

Caramelized Sea Scallops
~clementine-fennel relish

Clementine Marinade

1 tablespoon garlic, minced

3 tablespoons ginger, minced

3 tablespoons red jalapeño, seeded and minced

11 ounces fresh clementine juice

4 ounces rice wine vinegar

16 sea diver scallops, muscle removed

salt and white pepper, as needed

Clementine-Fennel Relish

3/4 teaspoon fennel seed

refined sunflower oil, as needed

9 ounces fennel, core removed and *julienne* (reserve fronds to garnish)

1 Granny Smith apple, pared, cored and *julienne*

3 ounces Spanish onion, *julienne*

1 1/2 tablespoon red jalapeño, seeded and minced

6 ounces fresh clementine juice

2 1/4 ounces rice wine vinegar

salt, to taste

16 clementine segments, to garnish

Procedure for Marinating Scallops:

Combine garlic, ginger, jalapeño, clementine juice, and vinegar in a lidded quart container; stir in scallops, cover, and marinate for two hours refrigerated.

Procedure for Clementine-Fennel Relish:

Heat an eight inch skillet over a low flame; add fennel seed, and lightly toast until aroma is released shaking pan frequently. Film skillet with oil, and heat over a medium-low flame; add fennel, apple, onion, and jalapeño, and *sweat. Increase flame to high, add juice and vinegar, and cook until liquid is absorbed stirring frequently; salt lightly to taste. Scrape relish into a microwavable container.

Procedure for Caramelized Scallops:

Pour marinated scallops through a sieve placed over a small saucepan. Transfer scallops to a large plate, and lightly season with salt and white pepper.

Bring marinade to a gentle boil, and cook until syrupy.

Heat an eight inch Teflon® sauté pan over a medium-high flame. Very lightly rub scallops with oil. Without crowding pan, *sear bottom of scallops until caramelized. Turn scallops, and cook for one additional minute. Transfer onto a clean plate tented with foil to retain heat; warm clementine-fennel relish briefly in microwave.

Plating:

Mound relish in the center of four warmed small plates, and garnish with a fennel frond. Encircle relish with alternating scallops and clementine segments. Drizzle with warm marinade.

Yield:

four servings

*julienne: to thinly slice to long, thin 1/8-inch rectangular strips

*sweat: to cook without color in a small amount of fat over a low flame

*sear: to brown the surface of food in fat over a high flame

Fettuccine Alfredo

salt, as needed

16 ounces heavy cream

5 ounces Parmigiano Reggiano, finely grated

10 ounces dried fettuccine pasta

white pepper, to taste

1 ounce unsalted butter, cold

parsley, finely chopped, to garnish

Procedure:

Three-fourths fill an eight quart pasta pot with cold water, and bring to the boil; salt the water to taste the salt.

Pour cream into a two quart saucepan, and place over a medium flame. Bring cream to a gentle boil, and cook until slightly thickened whisking occasionally.

Adjust flame to low-medium. Gradually add Parmigiano Reggiano whisking thoroughly to incorporate each addition. Adjust flame to low, and cook sauce briefly to develop flavor whisking frequently. Do *not* allow parmesan cream to simmer.

Cook fettuccine al dente stirring occasionally.

Season parmesan cream lightly with white pepper, and remove from heat. Thoroughly whisk in butter.

Drain fettuccine; do not rinse. Pour into pasta pot. Pour sauce over pasta and lift and separate to evenly distribute.

Plating:

Create nests by twirling fettuccine Alfredo with tongs onto four warmed square plates. Sprinkle with parsley.

Yield:

four servings

Gateau Escargot
~red wine gastrique

Red Wine Gastrique

75 milliliters soft red wine

150 milliliters oak aged red wine vinegar

1 small shallot, grated

1 ounce dark brown sugar

50 milliliters extra virgin olive oil

salt, to taste

Gateau Escargot

2 pounds medium zucchini, rinsed and dried

salt, as needed

olive oil, as needed

6 ounces baby Portobello mushrooms, cleaned and quartered

6 ounces shitake mushroom caps, cleaned and quartered

2 tablespoons shallots, minced

1 tablespoon garlic, minced

freshly ground black pepper, as needed

1/2 pound escargot, rinsed and drained

parsley, finely chopped, as needed

Procedure for Red Wine Gastrique:

Pour wine, vinegar, shallot, and sugar into a small bowl, and whisk until well combined.

Steadily whisk in oil to emulsify; very lightly season with salt.

Pour *gastrique* into a ten inch sauté pan, and reserve.

Procedure for Gateau Escargot:

Slice the skin 1/4-inch thick from zucchini using a *mandoline*. Wrap zucchini flesh in plastic, and refrigerate for another use.

Pour approximately two inches cold water into a two quart saucepan, and season to taste the salt. Half-fill a medium-sized bowl with ice and water.

Arrange zucchini slices loosely in a steamer basket. Bring seasoned water fully to the boil, insert basket, and cover. Briefly *blanch* slices until pliable. Immediately *shock* in ice bath; thoroughly drain.

Cover a baking sheet with parchment. Place four 4-inch flan rings on prepared pan. Line the bottom of rings with zucchini slices slightly overlapping and tucking snugly against the sides to form an even layer. Allow length of zucchini to drape over sides of rings.

Place a large skillet over a medium flame, and generously film with oil. *Sauté* mushrooms until golden brown; remove 4 tablespoons, season lightly, and reserve. Adjust flame to low, add shallot, and garlic, season with black pepper, and *sweat*. Remove skillet from heat. Stir in escargot, 3 tablespoons parsley, and season to taste.

Portion escargot mixture into prepared flan rings. Fold zucchini over mixture, and refrigerate until cold.

Preheat radiant oven to 400°.

Heat a ten inch Teflon® sauté pan over a medium-low flame, and film with oil. Using a large spatula place escargot gateaus (in flan rings) into pan, and cook until golden brown; turn gateaus, and cook until the other side is lightly golden. Add reserved mushrooms to pan, and place into oven for seven minutes to heat through.

Heat *gastrique* to a gentle boil over a medium flame stirring constantly until mixture is separated and syrupy. Remove from heat.

Plating:

Swirl 2 tablespoons *gastrique* onto four warmed small plates; center escargot gateaus, and carefully remove flan rings. Pile 1 tablespoon of mushrooms onto each gateau, and sprinkle with parsley.

Yield:

four servings

mandoline: a stainless slicer with blades adjustable for cut and thickness

blanch: to cook briefly in boiling water or hot fat

shock: to stop the cooking process

sauté: to cook quickly in a small amount of fat

sweat: to cook without color in a small amount of fat over a low flame

gastrique: a mixture of vinegar and sugar cooked to a syrupy consistency

Tourtière
~apricot-tomato jam

Pâte

2 cups unbleached all purpose flour

1/2 teaspoon salt

1/2 cup solid vegetable shortening, cold

2 tablespoons rendered lard, cold

1/3 cup ice cold water

pastry flour, as needed

Apricot-Tomato Jam

1 1/2 cup dried apricots, *julienne*

12 ounces apple juice

refined sunflower oil, as needed

3 tablespoons shallots, minced

1 1/2 teaspoon tomato paste

3 tablespoons apple cider vinegar

6 ounces tomato purée

3/4 teaspoon Coleman's® dry mustard

1/2 teaspoon ground ginger

dash Worcestershire sauce

Tourtière

1 1/4 pound white potatoes, peeled and *large dice* (weight after peeling)

salt and white pepper, to taste

4 slices cob-smoked bacon

1 1/2 pound ground pork

3/4 pound 75/25 ground beef

1 tablespoon unsalted butter

1 medium Spanish onion, *small dice*

2 stalks celery, *small dice*

2 teaspoons garlic, minced

freshly ground black pepper, as needed

1 tablespoon Bell's® seasoning

4 ounces **Veal Stock** (see recipe for **Veal Stock**, page 49)

1 egg combined with 1 tablespoon cold water for egg wash

Procedure for Pâte:

Pour flour and salt into food processor work bowl fitted with metal blade, and pulse on and off to combine.

Scatter shortening and lard by the tablespoon over flour mixture. Pulse on and off until a rough mixture begins to form. Do *not* over process.

Remove lid, sprinkle with water, and pulse on and off until pâte begins to leave sides of work bowl. Do *not* allow pâte to form a ball.

Pour pâte evenly onto two large sheets of plastic wrap. Using edges of plastic gather dough. Fold plastic over dough, flatten to discs, and place inside of a plastic bag. Refrigerate for three hours.

Generously dust a cold work surface with pastry flour. Place one unwrapped disc on work surface, and dust with flour. Keeping disc round roll to 10 x 1/8-inch. Carefully transfer pâte into a 9-inch pie plate leaving overhang untrimmed. Refrigerate. Roll remaining disc, lightly dust with flour, and place onto a parchment lined baking sheet. Cover with parchment, and refrigerate.

Procedure for Apricot-Tomato Jam:

Place apricots into a small saucepan, add apple juice, and bring to the boil. Remove pan from heat, cover, and steep for twenty minutes. Drain; reserve apricots and juice separately.

Heat an eight inch skillet over a low flame and film lightly with oil. Add shallots and tomato paste, and *sweat*. Stir in apricots. Adjust flame to medium-high, add vinegar, and reduce until syrupy stirring constantly. Add purée and reserved juice; bring to the boil, adjust flame to low, and simmer for twenty minutes stirring occasionally. Stir in dry mustard and ginger, and season with Worcestershire sauce. Remove jam from heat.

Procedure for Tourtière:

Pour potatoes into a three quart saucepan, cover with cold water, and salt the water to taste the salt; bring to the boil. Cook potatoes until tender yet not falling apart; drain thoroughly. Rice potatoes using a Foley food mill set over a medium-sized bowl; lightly season to taste.

Half fill a small saucepan with cold water, and bring to the boil; add bacon and *blanch* until water begins to boil. Drain, rinse with cold water, and pat dry. Chop bacon, add to a large skillet, and place over a low flame. Cook until fat is rendered, and bacon is crisped. Combine bacon with potatoes. Pour fat into a small cup, and reserve. Adjust flame to medium, stir in pork, and thoroughly cook stirring frequently. Transfer pork with a slotted spoon into bowl of potatoes. Add beef to skillet, and thoroughly cook stirring frequently. Transfer with slotted spoon into bowl of potatoes. Discard fat from skillet.

Return bacon fat to skillet, add butter, and reduce flame to low. Stir in onion, celery, garlic, black pepper, and Bell's® seasoning, and *sweat*. Adjust flame to high, add stock, and reduce until syrupy stirring frequently. Combine vegetables with potato mixture, and season generously. Allow mixture to cool to room temperature.

Preheat radiant oven to 375°.

Place pâte-lined pie plate on a baking sheet, and pile high with cooled mixture. Carefully cover with rolled pâte, and create a fork-fluted edging. Cut a tiny hole into top of tourtière for steam to escape. Lightly brush with egg wash.

Bake approximately forty to forty-five minutes until deeply golden brown.

Place tourtière on a rack. Cool for fifteen minutes before slicing.

Plating:

Offset a portion of apricot-tomato jam top right of center on a small plate. Slice and portion tourtière. Arrange slice left of center just below jam.

Yield:

ten servings

julienne: to thinly slice to long, thin 1/8-inch rectangular strips

large dice: to cut to 3/4-inch square

small dice: to cut to 1/4-inch square

sweat: to cook without color in a small amount of fat over a low flame

blanch: to cook briefly in boiling water or hot fat

❧

Vermont Cheddar Rolls

7 ounces warm water, 105°

1/4 ounce dry active yeast

1 teaspoon granulated sugar

3 ounces plain yogurt

10 ounces bread flour

2 ounces high-gluten flour

2 ounces semolina

2 ounces oat flour

1/2 teaspoon hot Hungarian paprika

1/2 teaspoon Coleman's® dry mustard

2 teaspoons salt

safflower oil, as needed

4 ounces Vermont mild white cheddar, grated

cornmeal, as needed

1 egg combined with 1 tablespoon cold water for egg wash

Procedure:

Pour 7 ounces water into a warmed 5-quart KitchenAid® mixer bowl, sprinkle in yeast and sugar, and whisk to combine. Allow yeast to *proof* for ten minutes.

Attach dough hook to mixer; add yogurt, bread flour, high-gluten flour, semolina, oat flour, paprika, and dry mustard. Begin *kneading* on Stir speed until dough begins to form; add salt. Steadily add 1 ounce oil. Adjust to speed 2, and add additional flour or water as needed to achieve a moist dough. *Knead* for five minutes. Gradually add cheddar, and continue to *knead* for two minutes. Turn dough out onto work surface, and *knead* until dough feels smooth and elastic.

Lightly oil a medium-sized bowl. Place dough into bowl, oiled side up, and cover with plastic wrap and a tea towel. Allow dough to rise in a warm area until doubled in bulk. Line a baking sheet with parchment, and dust with cornmeal.

Turn dough out onto work surface, and lightly flatten. Cover with a dampened tea towel, and rest for five minutes. Roll to *2 fold* dough. Cover with dampened tea towel, and rest five minutes.

Scale dough into two ounce portions. Working quickly *round* portions with dampened hands, and place on prepared baking sheet. Cover with dampened tea towel, and rise just until doubled in bulk.

Preheat radiant oven to 375°. Brush rolls with egg wash from bottom up to top, and cut one slash into tops. Bake for fifteen minutes, turn baking sheet, and continue to bake until deeply golden brown approximately twelve minutes. Cool completely on a rack. Heat rolls for five minutes in a preheated 350° oven to serve.

Yield:

fifteen rolls

proof: to allow yeast to rise

knead: to develop gluten in dough to expand and hold carbon dioxide

2 fold: Square flattened dough. Beginning at top of the dough, fold one-half down; gently seal seam. Bring bottom of dough up and over forming a log shape, and gently seal seam.

round: to shape dough into a tight, smooth ball

Rosemary-Raisin Baguettes

6 ounces warm water, 105°

1/4 ounce dry active yeast

1 1/2 ounce (scant) honey

1/2 tablespoon rosemary, chopped

1/4 cup and 1/4 pound bread flour, divided

1/2 pound whole wheat flour

1/4 cup unbleached all purpose flour, and additional for dusting

1/2 cup nonfat dry milk

1/2 tablespoon (scant) salt

extra virgin olive oil, as needed

1 large egg, room temperature

1/2 cup raisins, chopped

cornmeal, as needed

Procedure:

Pour 6 ounces water into a warmed 5-quart KitchenAid® mixer bowl, and whisk in yeast and honey. Allow yeast to *proof* for ten minutes.

Pour rosemary and 1/4 cup bread flour into food processor work bowl fitted with metal blade, and process to combine.

Attach dough hook to mixer; add rosemary flour, 1/4 pound bread flour, whole wheat flour, 1/4 cup all purpose flour, and dry milk to yeast mixture. *Knead* on speed Stir until dough begins to form. Add salt, and continue to *knead*. Combine 1 ounce oil with egg; steadily add to dough. Adjust to speed 2, and *knead* for seven minutes. Dough will be sticky. Add raisins, and *knead* for three minutes.

Turn dough out onto flour-dusted work surface, and finish *kneading* by hand until dough feels smooth and elastic.

Lightly oil a medium-sized bowl. Place dough into bowl, oiled side up, and cover with plastic wrap and a tea towel. Allow dough to rise in a warm area until doubled in bulk.

Line a baking sheet with parchment, and dust with cornmeal.

Turn dough out onto work surface. Flatten into a rectangle, cover with a dampened tea towel, and rest dough for five minutes.

Roll to *3 fold* dough. Cover with dampened tea towel, and rest for five minutes.

Scale dough into three, ten and one-half-ounce portions. Form each portion into a rectangle using a bench scraper to square edges.

Flatten first rectangle; turn top edge down one-half-inch, and form a tight seal. Roll into a log shape keeping each roll tight, and seal the final seam. Repeat the procedure with remaining rectangles, and cover with dampened tea towel.

With dampened palms placed on either side of the middle of first log, roll outward toward ends of log. Repeat the procedure with remaining logs, and cover with dampened tea towel.

Dampen palms, and roll the first shaped log outward to form a thin baguette with tapered ends. Center the baguette on prepared baking sheet. Repeat the procedure with remaining logs, and place on baking sheet. Cover with dampened tea towel. Allow baguettes to rise until nearly doubled in bulk.

Preheat radiant oven to 375°. Fill a cake pan with water, and place on lowest oven rack.

Brush baguettes with oil, and slash each diagonally three times. Place baking sheet on center oven rack, hit the cake pan to cause water to splash, and close oven door.

Bake for fifteen minutes, turn baking sheet, and bake approximately seven minutes until deeply golden brown. Cool completely on a rack.

Yield:

three baguettes

proof: to allow yeast to rise

knead: to develop gluten in dough to expand and hold carbon dioxide

3 fold: Square flattened dough. Beginning at the top of the dough, fold one-third down; gently seal seam. Repeat the fold. For the third fold, bring bottom of dough up and over forming a log shape; gently seal seam.

Crusty Boules

Sponge

6 ounces warm water, 105°
1/4 ounce dry active yeast
8 ounces bread flour

Rounds

all of sponge
dash dry active yeast
9 ounces warm water, 105°
1 pound bread flour, and additional for sifting
2 ounces high-gluten flour
3/4 tablespoon salt
olive oil, as needed
cornmeal, as needed

Procedure for Sponge:

Combine 6 ounces water, yeast, and bread flour in a warmed medium-sized bowl. Pull ingredients to a shaggy mass with a rubber dough scraper. Allow *sponge to stand at room temperature for fifteen minutes. Cover bowl with plastic wrap, and refrigerate overnight.

Procedure for Boules:

Allow *sponge to come to room temperature.

Pour *sponge, yeast, 9 ounces water, and bread and high-gluten flours into a 5-quart KitchenAid® mixer bowl, and attach dough hook. *Knead on speed Stir until dough comes together. Add salt, and turn to speed 2; add water as needed to achieve a moist dough. *Knead for nine minutes.

Turn dough out onto work surface, and continue *kneading by hand until dough feels smooth and elastic.

Lightly oil a medium-sized bowl. Place dough into bowl, oiled side up, and cover with plastic wrap and a tea towel. Allow dough to rise in a warm area until fully doubled in bulk.

Line a baking sheet with parchment, and dust with cornmeal.

Turn dough out onto work surface, and flatten. Cover with a dampened tea towel, and rest for five minutes.

Roll to *3 fold dough. Cover with dampened tea towel, and rest for five minutes.

Scale dough in three equal portions, place smooth side down on work surface, and flatten. With moistened hands, fold sides of portions into center, and seal forming circles. Flip portions over, and *round. Place equally spaced on prepared baking sheet, and cover with dampened tea towel. Allow boules to rise until fully doubled in bulk.

Preheat radiant oven to 425°. Fill a cake pan with water, and place on lowest oven rack.

Lightly sift bread flour over boules, and slash a cross hatch design into tops. Place baking sheet on center oven rack, hit the cake pan to cause water to splash, and close the door.

Bake for twenty minutes, turn, and continue to bake approximately ten minutes or until deeply golden brown, and bottoms sound hollow when tapped. Turn off oven, and slightly open door. Allow boules to remain in oven for five minutes to develop crust.

Cool completely on a rack.

Yield:

three boules

sponge: a thick yeast batter fermented to a spongy consistency

proof: to allow yeast to rise

knead: to develop gluten in dough to expand and hold carbon dioxide

3 fold: Square flattened dough. Beginning at top of the dough, fold one-third down; gently seal seam. Repeat the fold. For the third fold, bring bottom of dough up and over forming a log shape; gently seal seam.

round: to shape dough into a tight, smooth ball

Triple-Seeded Braid

7 ounces warm water, 105°

1/4 ounce dry active yeast

1/2 tablespoon granulated sugar

6 ounces high-gluten flour

6 ounces bread flour

1 ounce whole wheat flour

1/4 ounce malt powder

1 1/2 teaspoon salt

1 teaspoon *each* sesame seed, poppy seed, and flax seed,

and additional for sprinkling

safflower oil, as needed

1 egg combined with 1 tablespoon cold water for egg wash

Procedure:

Pour 7 ounces water into a warmed 5-quart KitchenAid® mixer bowl, and whisk in yeast and sugar. Allow yeast to *proof* for ten minutes.

Attach dough hook to mixer; add high-gluten, bread, and whole wheat flours, and malt powder to yeast mixture. *Knead* on speed Stir until dough begins to form. Add salt, and turn to speed 2. Add additional flour or water as needed to achieve a slightly moist dough. *Knead* for five minutes. Add 1 teaspoon each of sesame, poppy and flax seed, and *knead* for two minutes.

Turn dough out onto work surface, and continue *kneading* by hand until dough feels smooth and elastic.

Lightly oil a medium-sized bowl. Place dough into bowl, oiled side up, and cover with plastic wrap and a tea towel. Allow dough to rise in a warm area until doubled in bulk.

Gently press fist into dough to deflate, and rise again until nearly doubled in bulk. Line a baking sheet with parchment.

Turn dough out onto work surface, and flatten. Cover with a dampened tea towel, and rest for five minutes. Roll to *3 fold* dough. Cover with dampened tea towel and rest five minutes.

Scale dough into three equal portions. Form portions into rectangles using a bench scraper to square edges, and cover with dampened tea towel.

Flatten first rectangle; turn top edge down one-half-inch, and form a tight seal. Roll dough into a log shape keeping each roll tight, and seal the final seam. Repeat the procedure with remaining rectangles, and cover with dampened tea towel. With dampened palms placed on either side of the middle of the first log, roll outward toward the ends to form a 15-inch rope. Repeat the procedure with remaining logs.

Place ropes lengthwise on baking sheet. Without stretching, braid ropes from the middle to one end, fold end under, and pinch to seal. Turn baking sheet, and continue braiding from middle to end, fold end under, and pinch to seal.

Cover baking sheet with dampened tea towel. Allow braid to rise in a warm area until nearly doubled in bulk.

Preheat radiant oven to 375°.

Egg wash braid, and lightly sprinkle with seeds. Bake for forty minutes or until deeply golden brown, and bottom sounds hollow when tapped.

Place baking sheet on a rack to cool braid briefly. Transfer braid onto rack to cool completely.

Yield:

one braid

proof: to allow yeast to rise

knead: to develop gluten in dough to expand and hold carbon dioxide

3 fold: Square flattened dough. Beginning at top of the dough, fold one-third down; gently seal seam. Repeat the fold. For the third fold, bring bottom of dough up and over forming a log shape; gently seal seam.

෧

Mushroom Cream Soup

1 1/2 ounce dried wild mushroom blend

10 ounces cold water

1 quart **Chicken Stock** (see recipe for **Chicken Stock**, page 35)

3 1/2 ounces unsalted butter, divided

2 ounces unbleached all purpose flour

sachet d' épices tied in cheesecloth (3 parsley stems, 1/2 teaspoon dried thyme, 1 clove garlic, peeled, 1 bay leaf, and 3 black peppercorns)

8 ounces heavy cream

4 ounces baby Portobello mushrooms, cleaned and sliced

12 ounces button mushrooms, cleaned and sliced

1 1/2 large Spanish onion, *small dice*

2 stalks celery, *small dice*

2 teaspoons garlic, minced

1 tablespoon thyme leaves, chopped

freshly ground black pepper, as needed

1 ounce dry sherry

salt and cayenne, to taste

parsley, finely chopped, to garnish

Procedure:

Pour wild mushrooms into a small saucepan, cover with cold water, and bring to the boil. Cover pan, and remove from heat. Allow mushrooms to steep for twenty minutes. Strain through a fine sieve placed over a small bowl. Julienne mushrooms; reserve mushrooms and broth separately.

Pour chicken stock into a two quart saucepan. Bring stock to the boil, and remove from heat. Melt 1 1/2 ounce butter in a small stainless *rondeau* set over a low flame. Gradually stir in flour, evenly combine each addition. Cook *roux* for three minutes stirring occasionally. Steadily whisk stock into *roux*, and thoroughly combine to prevent lumping. Bring to the boil, reduce flame to low, add *sachet d' épices* and simmer *velouté* for thirty minutes stirring occasionally. Strain through a fine sieve into a large bowl, and reserve. Discard sachet.

Gently warm cream in a small saucepan set over a low flame. Wash *rondeau*; add remaining 2 ounces butter, and melt over a medium flame. Add fresh mushrooms, onion, celery, garlic, and thyme, season with black pepper, and cook until mushrooms are golden brown. Adjust flame to high, add mushroom broth, and stir until volume is reduced by half. Reduce flame to low, stir in *velouté*, and simmer for ten minutes. Strain through a sieve into a three quart saucepan. Press on vegetables to release juices. Purée vegetables; whisk into soup. Place saucepan over a low flame, whisk in cream, stir in wild mushrooms, and simmer for twenty minutes. Add sherry, and season to taste.

Plating:

Ladle soup into warmed deep bowls, and garnish with parsley.

Yield:

four servings

sachet d' épices: a small packet of aromatic spices

small dice: to cut to 1/4-inch square

julienne: to thinly slice to long, thin 1/8-inch rectangular strips

rondeau: a shallow, wide, straight-sided pot with handles

roux: a mixture of flour and butter used to thicken liquids

velouté: a sauce of white stock thickened with white roux

Cream of Parsnip

1 ounce unsalted butter

1 cup leek, white part only, well-rinsed and thinly sliced

9 ounces parsnips, peeled and *small dice* (weight after peeling)

4 ounces waxy potato, peeled and *small dice* (weight after peeling)

24 ounces **Chicken Stock** (see recipe for **Chicken Stock**, page 35)

12 ounces apple juice combined with 12 ounces cold water

8 ounces heavy cream

salt and white pepper, to taste

parsley, finely chopped, to garnish

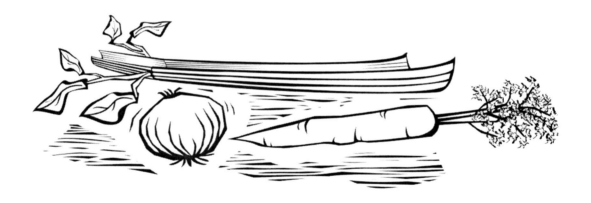

Procedure:

Heat a small *rondeau* over a low flame, add butter and melt. Add leek and parsnips, and *sweat* vegetables until softened. Add potato, and toss to combine. Stir in stock, combined apple juice and water, and bring to the boil. Adjust flame to low, and simmer stirring occasionally until vegetables are tender approximately thirty minutes.

Pour cream into a small saucepan, and gently warm over a low flame.

Strain vegetable mixture through a sieve placed over a medium-sized bowl; reserve liquid and vegetables separately. Purée vegetables until very smooth adding liquid as needed. Rinse *rondeau*, and pour in purée. Steadily whisk in liquid to fully incorporate. Place over a medium flame, and whisk in warmed cream. Cook to develop flavor and consistency, and season lightly to taste.

Plating:

Pour soup into warmed deep bowls. Garnish with a pinch of parsley.

Yield:

five servings

small dice: to cut to 1/4-inch square

rondeau: a shallow, wide, straight-sided pot with two loop handles

sweat: to cook without color in a small amount of fat over a low flame

Roasted Acorn Squash and Apple Bisque
~crème fraîche

Crème Fraîche

1 cup heavy cream

1 tablespoon buttermilk, fresh and well-shaken

Bisque

56 ounces **Chicken Stock** (see recipe for **Chicken Stock**, page 35)

2 small carrots, peeled and halved

1/2 large Spanish onion, thinly sliced

1 1/2 large acorn squash, halved and seeded

2 ounces unsalted butter, divided

2 1/2 large Cortland apples, peeled, cored and chopped

1 cinnamon stick

1 1/2 tablespoon grated ginger

4 ounces apple juice

1 teaspoon vanilla extract

pure Vermont maple syrup, as needed

salt and white pepper, to taste

2 tablespoons crystallized ginger, *julienne, to garnish

Procedure for Crème Fraîche:

Combine heavy cream and buttermilk by stirring in a clean glass jar with a lid. Place in a warm space in the kitchen, lidded and undisturbed, for thirty-six hours.

Refrigerate crème fraîche. It will continue to thicken and will remain fresh for one week. Lightly whisk to serve.

Procedure for Bisque:

Pour stock into a three quart saucepan, and bring to the boil; remove from heat, and reserve.

Preheat radiant oven to 350°.

Strew carrots and onion onto the bottom of a small roasting pan, and top with squash halves cut side up.

Heat an eight inch sauté pan over a medium flame, add 1 ounce butter and melt. Add apples, cinnamon, and ginger, and cook until apples are slightly softened stirring frequently. Adjust flame to high, add juice, and reduce until syrupy stirring constantly. Remove pan from heat; stir in vanilla and 5 tablespoons maple syrup.

Fill squash cavities with apple mixture, and dot with remaining butter. Pour enough stock into pan to reach one-third up the sides of squash. Cover pan tightly with foil, and roast for two hours. Allow squash to cool slightly. Scoop squash mixture into a medium-sized *rondeau*, and pour in pan stock. Add remaining stock, and bring to the boil. Adjust flame to low, and simmer for one hour stirring occasionally. Remove cinnamon stick, and purée bisque. Return bisque to *rondeau*, and place over a low flame. Stir in cold water as needed for consistency, and season to achieve an underlying sweetness; heat through.

Plating:

Ladle bisque into warmed deep bowls. Swirl in a tablespoon of crème fraîche, and sprinkle with crystallized ginger.

Yield:

eight servings

julienne: to thinly slice to long, thin 1/8-inch rectangular strips

rondeau: a shallow, wide, straight-sided pot with handles

Billi Bi Soup

Fish Fumet

1/2 pound white fish bones

1 medium Spanish onion, *small dice*

1 stalk celery with leaves, *small dice*

1/4 teaspoon saffron threads

1/4 teaspoon red pepper flakes

3 sprigs fresh parsley

6 white peppercorns

1 bay leaf

48 ounces cold water

Billi Bi Soup

3 pounds Maine farm-raised mussels

salt, as needed

1 quart fish *fumet (see Procedure)

1 pint dry white wine

1/2 cup shallots, sliced

1 large clove garlic, crushed

2 sprigs parsley

2 white peppercorns, cracked

pinch saffron threads

1 ounce unsalted butter

1 1/2 ounce unbleached all purpose flour

*sachet d' épices tied in cheesecloth (3 parsley stems, 1/2 teaspoon dried thyme, 1 clove garlic, peeled, 1 small bay leaf, and 3 white peppercorns)

8 ounces heavy cream

salt and white pepper, to taste

parsley, finely chopped, to garnish

Procedure for Fish Fumet:

Add fish *fumet ingredients into a medium-sized stainless *rondeau, and bring to the boil. Adjust flame to low, and simmer for forty-five minutes; skim and discard impurities from the surface. Do *not* stir.

Strain fish *fumet through a sieve into a medium-sized bowl; discard solids. Pour *fumet into *rondeau.

Procedure for Billi Bi Soup:

Scrub mussels under cold running water to remove dirt and beards. Pour into a large bowl filled with cold water and a dash of salt. Allow to soak for one hour to release sand. Drain, rinse; discard opened mussels.

Add wine, shallots, garlic, parsley, white peppercorns, and saffron to fish *fumet*, and bring to the boil; add mussels, and cover *rondeau*. Boil covered for approximately four minutes until mussel shells open. Discard unopened mussels. Transfer mussels into a large bowl with a slotted spoon. Strain mussel broth through a fine sieve double lined with cheesecloth into a three quart saucepan. Remove mussels from shells, place into a lidded container, cover and refrigerate. Bring broth to the boil, and remove from heat.

Rinse *rondeau*, and place over a low flame; add butter and melt. Gradually stir flour into butter, evenly combine each addition. Cook for three minutes stirring frequently. Steadily whisk mussel broth into *roux*, and thoroughly incorporate to prevent lumping. Bring to the boil, adjust flame to low, add *sachet d' épices* and simmer *velouté* for thirty minutes stirring occasionally.

Pour heavy cream into a small saucepan, and warm over a low flame. Strain *velouté* through a fine sieve into three quart saucepan; discard *sachet d' épices*. Place saucepan over a low flame, whisk in heavy cream, and simmer soup to develop flavor and consistency. Stir in mussels, season to taste, and heat through.

Plating:

Ladle billi bi into four warmed deep bowls. Garnish with parsley.

Yield:

four servings

small dice: to cut to 1/4-inch square

fumet: a highly flavored broth of aromatic ingredients and wine

sachet d' épices: a small packet of aromatic spices

rondeau: a shallow, wide, straight-sided pot with handles

roux: a mixture of flour and butter used to thicken liquids

velouté: a sauce of white stock thickened with white roux

❧

Spinach Salad with Honeyed Spiked Pecans and Gorgonzola
~cranberry vinaigrette

Cranberry Vinaigrette

1 ounce fresh cranberries

1 ounce fresh orange juice

1 teaspoon orange zest, minced

1 teaspoon granulated sugar

1 small shallot, minced

1 1/2 ounce frozen cranberry juice concentrate

2 ounces rice wine vinegar

1 1/2 ounce dry white wine

3 ounces safflower oil

2 ounces olive oil

salt and freshly ground black pepper, to taste

Honeyed Spiked Pecans

3 tablespoons honey

3 teaspoons hot water

1/2 teaspoon New Mexico red chile powder

dash *each* cloves, nutmeg, and cayenne

1 cup pecan halves

Salad

4 ounces leaf spinach, stemmed and torn bite-sized

1 1/2 ounce red onion, *julienne*

2 ounces sun dried cranberries

salt and freshly ground black pepper, to taste

2 ounces Gorgonzola, crumbled

Procedure for Cranberry Vinaigrette:

Pour fresh cranberries and orange juice into a small saucepan, stir in zest and sugar, and bring to a low boil over a medium flame. Cook until berries have popped and are quite softened stirring frequently. Cool mixture to room temperature.

Pour cranberry mixture, shallot, and concentrate into food processor work bowl fitted with metal blade, and process until puréed. Add vinegar and wine; process briefly.

Combine oils. With machine running, slowly add oil to emulsify; season lightly to taste. Pour into a lidded jar, cover, and refrigerate.

Procedure for Honeyed Spiked Pecans:

Preheat radiant oven to 350°.

Line a small baking sheet with parchment.

Combine honey, water, and spices in a small bowl; stir in pecans. Spread nuts and honeyed water mixture onto prepared baking sheet.

Bake for five minutes, turn, and continue to bake until pecans are deeply golden brown checking frequently.

Transfer honeyed spiked pecans onto a clean sheet of parchment. Separate nuts, cool completely, and roughly chop.

Procedure for Salad:

Rinse, and spin-dry spinach. Combine spinach, onion, and dried cranberries in a medium-sized bowl. Cover with dampened tea towel, and refrigerate.

Plating:

Whisk vinaigrette. Season salad, and dress lightly with vinaigrette; toss to coat. Mound on chilled plates, and scatter honeyed spiked pecans and gorgonzola.

Yield:

four servings

*julienne: to thinly slice to long, thin 1/8-inch rectangular strips

Buffalo Mozzarella, Wild Mushroom, and Vine-Ripened Tomato Salad

8 small cloves garlic, peeled

3 shallots, peeled

5 1/2 ounces olive oil

infused olive oil (see Procedure)

2 ounces cèpe mushroom caps, cleaned and *julienne*

4 ounces lobster mushrooms, cleaned and quartered

4 ounces cremini mushrooms, cleaned and halved

freshly ground black pepper, as needed

2 1/2 ounces dry white wine

2 1/2 teaspoons fresh lemon juice

1 teaspoon tarragon leaves, chopped

1 tablespoon parsley, chopped

salt, to taste

1 large vine ripened tomato

4 ounces farm produced buffalo mozzarella

1 ounce tarragon vinegar

Procedure:

Place garlic and shallots into a small saucepan, cover with 5 1/2 ounces olive oil, and bring to the boil; remove from heat, and cool to room temperature. Strain infused olive oil into a small glass measure cup. Chop garlic and shallots.

Heat 2 1/2 ounces infused olive oil in a ten inch sauté pan placed over a medium-high flame. Add mushrooms, season with pepper, and *sauté; stir in garlic and shallots. Immediately add wine and lemon juice, adjust flame to high, and stir until liquid is evaporated. Remove skillet from heat, and allow mixture to cool to room temperature. Stir in tarragon and parsley; season to taste.

Slice both the tomato and buffalo mozzarella into eight even slices.

Pour tarragon vinegar into a small bowl. Steadily whisk remaining infused oil into vinegar to emulsify; season to taste.

Plating:

Arrange alternating slices of tomato and mozzarella on four square plates. Mound mushroom mixture, centered, over slices. Drizzle with vinaigrette, and grind generously with black pepper.

Yield:

four servings

*julienne: to thinly slice to long, thin 1/8-inch rectangular strips

*sauté: to cook quickly in a small amount of fat

Salad of Smoked Turkey and Pecan Rice
~orange-balsamic vinaigrette

Orange-Balsamic Vinaigrette

3/4 ounce frozen orange juice concentrate

1/2 teaspoon orange zest, grated

2 teaspoons white onion, grated

3/4 ounce balsamic vinegar

1 ounce dry white wine

1 1/3 ounce peanut oil

1 1/2 ounce safflower oil

1/2 ounce olive oil

dash salt

Salad

2 cups packaged pecan rice, cooked and cooled

2 teaspoons unsalted butter

1/3 cup pecans, chopped

dash cayenne

salt, as needed

2 ounces snow peas, strings removed

3 tablespoons orange zest, *julienne*

1/2 cup peeled celery, *small dice*

1/2 cup Macoun apple, cored and *small dice*

1/4 cup white onion, *small dice*

8 ounces smoked turkey leg, *medium dice*

freshly ground black pepper, to taste

6 large radicchio leaves

Procedure for Orange-Balsamic Vinaigrette:

Pour concentrate, zest, onion, vinegar, and wine into food processor work bowl fitted with metal blade, and process to combine.

Combine oils. With machine running, slowly add oil to emulsify, and season lightly. Pour into a lidded jar, cover, and refrigerate.

Procedure for Salad:

Pour pecan rice into a medium-sized bowl. Heat a small sauté pan over a medium flame, add butter and melt. Scatter pecans, add cayenne, and toss frequently until lightly golden brown. Toss with rice to combine, and lightly season.

Pour approximately two inches of cold water into a two quart saucepan, season lightly with salt. Fill a small bowl with ice and water. Arrange snow peas loosely in a steamer basket. Bring seasoned water to the boil, insert basket, and cover. *Blanch peas until emerald green, and crisp to the bite. Immediately *shock in ice bath, and remove. *Blanch orange zest for ten seconds; drain, *shock, drain, and mince zest. Dry snow peas, and *julienne.

Combine snow peas, celery, apple, onion, and turkey with pecan rice. Season salad, and lightly dress with vinaigrette; toss to coat.

Plating:

Drizzle vinaigrette onto six cold large plates. Center radicchio leaves, and fill with salad. Sprinkle with orange zest.

Yield:

six servings

*julienne: to thinly slice to long, thin 1/8-inch rectangular strips

*small dice: to cut to 1/4-inch square

*medium dice: to cut to 1/3-inch square

*blanch: to cook briefly in boiling water or hot fat

*shock: to stop the cooking process

Red Bartlett Pear and Fontina Cheese Salad

Pear Vinaigrette

1 ounce pear nectar

1/2 ounce dry white wine

1/2 ounce champagne vinegar

1/2 tablespoon shallot, minced

1/4 teaspoon freshly ground black pepper

2 ounces almond oil

1 ounce safflower oil

dash salt

Caramelized Almonds

2 tablespoons sugar

2 ounces sliced almonds

Salad

2 ripe red Bartlett pears, cored and *small dice*

1 ounce sweet onion, *julienne*

3 ounces frisée, rinsed, spin-dried, and torn bite-sized

3 ounces Fontina, *small dice* and room temperature

16 large Belgian endive leaves

Procedure for Pear Vinaigrette:

Pour nectar, wine, and vinegar into food processor work bowl fitted with metal blade; add shallot and black pepper, and process to combine.

Combine oils. With machine running, add oil to emulsify, and season lightly. Pour into a lidded jar, cover, and refrigerate.

Procedure for Caramelized Almonds:

Pour sugar into a cold eight inch sauté pan, and scatter with almonds. Adjust flame to high, and shake pan constantly until sugar melts and nuts begin to caramelize. Immediately scrape almonds onto a sheet of parchment using a rubber spatula. Quickly separate into an even layer. Cool nuts completely.

Procedure for Salad:

Combine pears, onion, and frisée in a small bowl. Cover salad with dampened tea towel, and refrigerate briefly.

Plating:

Lightly dress salad with vinaigrette; toss to coat. Fold in half of caramelized almonds, and Fontina. Arrange endive leaves in a petal design on four chilled large plates. Pile salad into center of leaves. Scatter remaining almonds.

Yield:

four servings

small dice: to cut to 1/4-inch square

julienne: to thinly slice to long, thin 1/8-inch rectangular strips

ço

Coq au Vin

4 ounces salt pork

4 chicken thighs

4 chicken legs

salt and freshly ground black pepper, as needed

12 ounces cremini mushrooms, cleaned and halved

refined sunflower oil, as needed

6 ounces pearl onions, cooked

1 1/2 large Spanish onion, *small dice*

4 cloves garlic, minced

1 tablespoon thyme leaves, chopped

2 tablespoons Wondra® flour

8 ounces Côte du Nuits Burgundy wine

24 ounces **Chicken Stock** (see recipe for **Chicken Stock**, page 35)

sachet d' épices tied in cheesecloth (3 parsley stems, 1/2 teaspoon dried thyme, 1 clove garlic, peeled, 1 bay leaf, and 3 black peppercorns)

parsley, finely chopped, to garnish

Procedure:

Place salt pork into a two quart saucepan, cover with cold water, and bring to the boil. Adjust flame to low, simmer for ten minutes, and drain. Rinse pork well with cold water, dry, and *small dice*. Toss salt pork into a large *rondeau*, and place over a low-medium flame. Render fat and crisp pork; transfer pork into a medium-sized bowl. Adjust flame to medium-high.

Season chicken, add to *rondeau* in batches, and *sear* until evenly golden brown. Transfer chicken to a large plate. Add mushrooms into *rondeau*, season lightly with black pepper, and stir frequently until golden brown. Transfer mushrooms into bowl with pork. Add oil as needed, and stir in pearl onions; lightly caramelize, and add to bowl with pork. Adjust flame to low, stir in onion, garlic, and thyme, and *sweat*.

Sprinkle flour evenly over vegetables. Stir mixture for three minutes. Adjust flame to medium; steadily add wine, and reduce volume by two-thirds stirring constantly. Add stock, *sachet d' épices*, and reserved chicken; adjust flame to high, and bring to the boil. Adjust flame to low, partially cover *rondeau*, and simmer until chicken is cooked approximately thirty-five minutes. Skim and discard surface impurities. Transfer chicken into bowl with pork. Adjust flame to medium; reduce sauce to achieve depth of flavor and consistency. Remove *sachet d' épices*, and discard. Stir in chicken, pearl onions, mushrooms, pork and accumulated juices. Simmer coq au vin until heated through. Adjust seasoning as needed.

Plating:

Crisscross two pieces of chicken in the center of warmed bowls, and ladle generously with vegetables and sauce. Garnish with parsley, and accompany with Côte du Nuits.

Yield:

four servings

small dice: to cut to 1/4-inch square

sachet d' épices: a small packet of aromatic spices

sear: to brown the surface of food in fat over a high flame

rondeau: a shallow, wide, straight-sided pot with handles

sweat: to cook without color in a small amount of fat over a low flame

Crispy Magret of Duckling with Fresh Cranberry Compote
~creamy wild rice

Fresh Cranberry Compote

1/2 cup fresh lime juice

1/2 cup fresh orange juice

1/2 cup granulated sugar

1 tablespoon lime zest, *julienne*

1 tablespoon orange zest, *julienne*

1 tablespoon ginger, peeled and grated

1 cinnamon stick

dash cayenne

1/4 cup honey

12 ounces fresh cranberries

1/2 cup golden raisins

Creamy Wild Rice

1 cup Canadian wild rice

24 ounces cold water

5 ounces heavy cream

1 tablespoon unsalted butter

1/2 cup Spanish onion, *small dice*

1/4 cup red bell pepper, *small dice*

1/4 cup carrot, *small dice*

5 ounces heavy cream

salt and freshly ground black pepper, to taste

Crispy Magret of Duckling

1 3/4 pound farm-raised duckling *magret*, cut into four portions

salt and freshly ground black pepper, as needed

refined sunflower oil, as needed

Procedure for Cranberry Compote:

Pour juices and sugar into a three quart saucepan. Bring to the boil over a medium flame; stir often until sugar dissolves and mixture begins to thicken approximately five minutes.

Stir in zests, ginger, cinnamon, cayenne, honey, and cranberries, and bring to the boil. Boil compote until nearly half the berries have popped; stir in raisins, and remove from heat.

Compote will thicken as it cools.

Procedure for Creamy Rice:

Pour rice into a sieve, and rinse with cold water. Add rice and 24 ounces cold water into a three quart saucepan; bring to the boil, reduce flame to medium, and cook until grains begin to pop and rice is tender approximately fifty-two minutes. Remove saucepan from heat.

Heat a ten inch sauté pan over a low flame, add butter and melt. Add onion, red pepper, and carrot; *sweat* vegetables. Adjust flame to medium, add cream, and cook until thickened stirring frequently. Remove pan from heat.

Procedure for Crispy Magret of Duckling and Finishing Creamy Rice:

Preheat radiant oven to 400°.

Set two, eight inch cast-iron skillets over a medium-high flame, and heat until very hot. Place an empty can next to each skillet to collect drained fat.

Score the skin of each portion of *magret* with three parallel cuts, and season.

Film skillets very lightly with oil, and place two portioned *magret* skin side down into each skillet to *sear*. Drain fat immediately as it accumulates, and *sear* skin until deeply golden brown; turn *magret*, and briefly *sear* flesh side. Place skillets into oven, and roast to an internal temperature of 140° for medium-rare approximately twelve minutes. Transfer to a cutting board to rest briefly.

Stir creamed vegetables into wild rice. Place saucepan over a low flame, and stir until heated through; season to taste.

Plating:

Diagonally slice *magret* portions. Spoon cranberry compote onto left half of four large warmed plates. Overlap *magret* slices on compote forming a half circle. Tuck in a mound of creamy rice.

Yield:

four servings

julienne: to thinly slice to long, thin 1/8-inch rectangular strips

small dice: to cut to 1/4-inch square

magret: a lean portion of meat from the breast of a fattened duckling with the skin and underlying layer of fat attached

sweat: to cook without color in a small amount of fat over a low flame

sear: to brown the surface of food in fat over a high flame

Wiener Schnitzel
~potato pancakes and red cabbage

Red Cabbage

3 ounces unsalted butter

1 1/2 pound red cabbage, cored and roughly shredded

2 Greening apples, peeled and shredded (Granny Smith may be substituted)

2 tablespoons lemon marmalade

4 tablespoons honey

4 ounces fresh lemon juice

4 ounces black currant vinegar

salt and freshly ground black pepper, to taste

Potato Pancakes

1 extra large egg

1 ounce parsley, finely chopped

4 ounces Spanish onion, *small dice

3 1/2 pounds russet potatoes, peeled and held in cold water

unbleached all purpose flour, as needed

granulated garlic, salt, and white pepper to taste

refined sunflower oil, as needed

Wiener Schnitzel

1/2 pound veal top round

salt and freshly ground black pepper, as needed

1/4 cup unbleached all purpose flour

1 extra large egg, beaten

2/3 cup dried breadcrumbs

refined sunflower oil, as needed

*clarified butter, as needed

4 thin slices lemon, twisted into an S shape, to garnish

Procedure for Red Cabbage:

Heat a large *rondeau* over a medium flame, add butter and melt. Stir in cabbage and apples, cover, and cook cabbage until barely tender stirring frequently. Uncover, add marmalade and honey and combine well.

Increase flame to high, and add lemon juice and vinegar. Stir cabbage mixture constantly until liquid is nearly evaporated. Remove from heat, season to taste, and cover.

Procedure for Potato Pancakes:

Combine egg, parsley, and onion in a small bowl.

Hand grate potatoes into a colander placed inside of a large bowl. Press on potatoes to extract liquid; discard liquid but save the thin layer of potato starch accumulated in bowl. Toss the potatoes with the starch.

Stir 1/2 ounce of flour into potatoes. Squeeze a handful of potatoes: if potatoes don't hold together add additional flour as needed. Season generously to taste; stir egg mixture into potatoes combining well.

Heat a ten inch cast-iron skillet over a medium flame; add 1/2 inch oil, and thoroughly heat.

Portion potato mixture with a solid kitchen spoon, and squeeze out liquid. Ease into hot oil, and flatten pancake with back of spoon. Add additional pancakes to skillet without crowding. Cook until golden on both sides. Move pancakes frequently in hot oil. Transfer to a rack-lined baking sheet. Continue procedure with remaining mixture, adding and heating oil as needed.

Procedure for Wiener Schnitzel and Finishing Potato Pancakes:

Slice veal across the grain into two ounce portions. Place between two sheets of plastic, and pound to 1/4-inch thickness with the smooth side of a meat mallet. Place veal on a rack-lined baking sheet, and season.

Place flour, egg, and breadcrumbs each into pie tins. Dredge veal in flour; shake off excess. Coat with egg, and press on breadcrumbs. Place veal back on rack, and refrigerate for one hour. Discard unused breading.

Preheat radiant oven to 325°. Bake potato pancakes for twenty minutes. Heat red cabbage, uncovered, over a low flame.

Heat two ten inch cast-iron skillets over a medium flame. Pour 1/2-inch of oil and *clarified butter* combined into each skillet, and thoroughly heat. Place two slices of veal into each skillet. *Pan-fry* until golden brown on both sides. Move veal frequently in hot fat. Remove skillets from heat, and serve immediately.

Plating:

Spoon a mound of cabbage, centered, near the rim of four large warmed plates. Lean three pancakes against cabbage, and lean veal against pancakes. Garnish with lemon twist.

Yield:

four servings

small dice: to cut to 1/4-inch square

clarified butter. To remove milk solids and water from butter: melt butter in a heavy saucepan over a low flame until milk solids fall to the bottom of the pan; discard foam from the surface, and pour butterfat into a small bowl leaving milk solids in bottom of pan. Discard solids.

rondeau: a shallow, wide, straight-sided pot with loop handles

pan-fry: to cook coated food in a skillet of hot oil over a medium flame

Venison Loin Roast with Sun-Dried Cherry Sauce
~sweet potato hash

Loin Roast with Sun-Dried Cherry Sauce

2 1/2 ounces sun-dried cherries

4 ounces Pinot Noir wine

3 pounds farm-raised venison deer loin, trimmed and tied

1 clove garlic, peeled and halved

freshly ground black pepper, as needed

olive oil, as needed

salt, as needed

2 ounces unsalted butter, cold and divided

2 tablespoons shallots, minced

2 tablespoons jalapeño, minced

16 ounces **Veal Stock** (see recipe for **Veal Stock**, page 49)

1/2 teaspoon arrowroot combined with 1 teaspoon cold water for *slurry*

2 x 1-inch strip orange zest

1 teaspoon black currant vinegar

Sweet Potato Hash

4 ounces unsalted butter

5 small baked sweet potatoes, peeled, *medium dice* and chilled

2 tablespoons Spanish onion, *medium dice*

2 tablespoons poblano pepper, *medium dice*

1/2 teaspoon New Mexico red chile powder

dash salt

Procedure for Loin Roast with Sun-Dried Cherry Sauce:

Combine cherries and wine in a small bowl, and cover with plastic wrap. Soften cherries at room temperature for two hours. Strain through a sieve placed over a small bowl. Reserve cherries and wine separately.

Rub loin with cut garlic, and season with black pepper. Rub lightly with oil. Allow to stand at room temperature for thirty minutes. Preheat radiant oven to 400°. Heat a ten inch cast-iron skillet over a medium-high flame and film with oil. Season loin with salt, and *sear* evenly until golden. Roast to an internal temperature of 125° for medium-rare. Transfer loin to a baking sheet, and tent lightly with foil. Place skillet over a medium flame, add 1 ounce butter and melt. Add shallots and jalapeño, season with black pepper, and lightly caramelize stirring frequently. Adjust flame to medium-high, stir in reserved wine, and reduce until syrupy stirring constantly. Stir *slurry*. Whisk stock, *slurry*, zest, and accumulated venison juices into skillet. Skim and discard surface impurities, and reduce sauce to a thin consistency. Adjust flame to medium-low, add cherries, and simmer to develop consistency and flavor stirring occasionally. Remove from heat.

Procedure for Sweet Potato Hash and Finishing Sauce:

Place a ten inch sauté pan over a medium-low flame, and add butter. Cook butter until water evaporates, adjust flame to high, and cook until hazelnut brown. Add potatoes, and toss until caramelized. Adjust flame to medium, add onion and poblano, season, and cook until onion is soft.

Warm sauce over a low flame; remove zest, whisk in vinegar and remaining ounce butter. Adjust seasoning, and remove from heat. Transfer loin to a cutting board, and slice evenly into twelve slices.

Plating:

Spoon sweet potato hash in the center of four large warmed plates, and drape with loin slices, slightly overlapping. Ladle sauce over loin, and evenly distribute cherries. Accompany entrée with Pinot Noir.

Yield:

four servings

slurry: a starch and cool liquid paste, cooked and used as a thickener

medium dice: to cut to 1/3-inch square

sear: to brown the surface of food in fat over a high flame

൧

Crème Caramel

1/2 cup granulated sugar

1/2 liter half-and-half

1/2 vanilla bean

100 grams granulated sugar

3 large egg yolks, room temperature

2 large eggs, room temperature

Chantilly Cream, to garnish (see recipe for **Chantilly Cream**, page 122)

Procedure:

Line a small shallow roasting pan with a single layer of paper towels, and set four 6-ounce glass ramekins inside. Place pan next to stove. Place measured 1/2 cup sugar next to stove.

Preheat radiant oven to 325°. Fill a kettle with water, and bring to the boil. Tear small slits into a sheet of aluminum foil sized to cover the roasting pan.

Heat an eight inch flat-bottomed sauté pan over a medium flame (pan is thoroughly hot when a pinch of sugar caramelizes in two seconds). When pan is heated, sprinkle a thin even layer of measured sugar over bottom of pan. Cook sugar until melted without swirling. Continue to sprinkle pan with thin even layers of sugar, working quickly and cooking each layer just until melted. Cook sugar to a deep caramel color. Immediately distribute cooked caramel evenly between ramekins.

Pour half-and-half into a small saucepan, and place over a low flame.

Scrape soft interior of vanilla bean into 100 grams sugar. Place pod inside of your sugar jar for flavor if desired, or discard.

Pour yolks, eggs, and vanilla sugar into a medium-sized bowl, and whisk until thickened and pale yellow.

Steadily stir warmed half-and-half into egg mixture without aeration. Strain through a fine sieve into a one quart glass measure cup. Pour custard into caramel-lined ramekins.

Pour boiled water into roasting pan to reach halfway up the sides of ramekins, and place into oven. Lightly place slit sheet of foil over pan.

Bake crèmes until custard is set approximately fifty minutes.

Remove crèmes from water, and place on a rack to cool completely. Wrap each ramekin with plastic, and refrigerate overnight.

Plating:

Insert a hot, dry paring knife perpendicular to side of ramekin. Evenly encircle ramekin to release crème. Tilt crème over the center of a dessert plate with a recessed rim, and gently pull crème away from sides with fingertips until suction is released. Place ramekin upside down onto crème. Repeat procedure with remaining crèmes. Carefully remove ramekins. Garnish pool of caramel with chantilly cream.

Yield:

four crème caramel

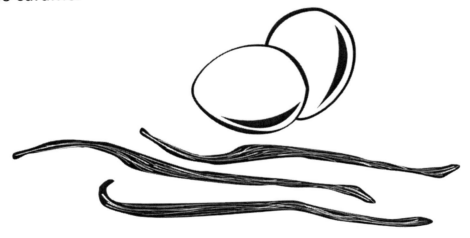

White Chocolate Cheesecake
~pomegranate sauce

Graham Cracker Crust

8 ounces graham cracker crumbs

6 ounces granulated sugar

3 ounces unsalted butter, melted

pan spray, as needed

White Chocolate Cheesecake

1/2 pound Callebaut® white chocolate, chopped

1 1/2 pound cream cheese, room temperature

3 ounces granulated sugar

1/2 pound sour cream

4 large eggs, room temperature

2 large egg yolks, room temperature

1/2 tablespoon vanilla extract

1 1/4 ounce cornstarch, sifted

Pomegranate Sauce (recipe follows **White Chocolate Cheesecake**)

4 tablespoons pomegranate seeds, to garnish

Procedure for Graham Cracker Crust:

Combine crumbs and sugar in a medium-sized bowl. Add melted butter, and mix until ingredients ball together when squeezed.

Preheat radiant oven to 350°. Place oven rack in third lowest position.

Lightly pan spray the bottom of an 8 x 3-inch cake pan. Place an 8-inch parchment circle onto bottom, and lightly spray parchment and sides of pan. Press a thin layer of crust mixture onto sides of pan to reach three-fourths up from bottom. Form a thin bottom layer. Press fingertips where bottom meets the sides of pan, ensuring a thin seal.

Place pan on a baking sheet, and bake crust for ten minutes. Cool crust completely on a rack. Do not turn off oven.

Procedure for White Chocolate Cheesecake:

Half fill a three quart saucepan with water, and place over a low flame. Pour chocolate into a flat-bottomed medium-sized stainless bowl, and set over saucepan to melt. Stir to combine. Remove saucepan from heat. Leave chocolate bowl on top of saucepan.

Place cream cheese into a 5-quart KitchenAid® mixer bowl, and attach flat beater. Blend on Stir speed until cheese is very smooth. With mixer running gradually add sugar, incorporate each addition. Add sour cream, and combine well. Add warm chocolate in a steady stream. Turn off mixer to scrape down bowl and beater.

Combine eggs, yolks, and vanilla extract. With mixer running on speed Stir gradually add egg mixture, fully incorporate each addition. Add sifted cornstarch, and blend just until incorporated.

Pour batter into cooled crust. Line a 12 x 10 x 6-inch hotel pan with a layer of paper towels, and set cheesecake into pan. Carefully pour hot water into hotel pan to reach halfway up sides of cheesecake pan. Place hotel pan on third lowest oven rack, and cover with a baking sheet. Bake cheesecake for one hour. Remove baking sheet, and continue to bake for approximately forty minutes, or until cheesecake slightly wobbles and top has domed.

Remove cheesecake from water, and place on a rack to cool completely. Wrap pan with plastic, and refrigerate overnight.

Place cheesecake over a medium-high flame and spin constantly until pan is warm to the touch; remove from heat. Insert an offset spatula perpendicular to side of pan, and evenly encircle pan to release cheesecake. Place a 9-inch cake circle over pan, and invert. Carefully remove pan and parchment. Place another cake circle onto cheesecake, and re-invert.

Plating:

Slice cheesecake into desired portions using a hot, dry, thin knife. Center slice on colorful dessert plate, and drizzle with pomegranate sauce. Garnish with fresh pomegranate seeds.

Yield:

ten servings

Pomegranate Sauce

340 grams pomegranate seeds

85 grams granulated sugar

heel of small lemon

Procedure:

Combine seeds and sugar in a small bowl, and cover with plastic wrap. Allow mixture to soften at room temperature for approximately one hour until sugar melts, stirring occasionally.

Pour mixture into food processor work bowl fitted with metal blade; process to blend scraping blade occasionally to dislodge seeds. The mixture will not be smooth. Pour through a sieve placed over a small saucepan, and press on seeds to extract juices. Discard seeds.

Place saucepan over a low flame, add lemon heel, and stir until a line drawn with fingertip on a rubber spatula remains. Pomegranate sauce will be thin.

Discard lemon heel. Cool sauce to room temperature. Pour into a plastic bottle with a tip, and refrigerate. Sauce will thicken as it chills.

Yield:

five ounces

Tarte Tatin
~vanilla bean ice cream

8 large Cortland apples, pared, cored, and cut evenly into quarters

2 ounces unsalted butter

2 1/2 cups granulated sugar

1 sheet prepared puff pastry, thawed, unfolded, and cold

pastry flour, as needed

1 egg combined with 1 tablespoon cold water for egg wash

Vanilla Bean Ice Cream (recipe follows **Tarte Tatin**)

Procedure:

Heat a ten inch sauté pan over a medium-low flame, add butter and melt. Pour sugar evenly over bottom of pan; remove from heat. Place one layer of apples, cut side up, to fit snugly over sugar. Add another layer in between the placed apples, cut side down, and position apples snugly in center of pan. Place over a medium-low flame, and cook until sugar begins to bubble around edges and apples are soft approximately forty-five minutes. Re-position pan occasionally to evenly caramelize sugar.

Preheat radiant oven to 425°. Place puff pastry on a lightly floured cold surface. Dust pastry with flour, and gently roll to a 10-inch circle. Remove pan of caramelized apples from heat, and cover with pastry; trim to fit. Egg wash, and slash three times to vent steam. Place pan on a baking sheet. Bake tarte for fifteen minutes, or until pastry is golden brown. Cool briefly on a rack. Refrigerate until cold. Place cold pan of tarte tatin over a medium flame and move pan constantly until sugar bubbles and tarte moves. Place a 10-inch cake circle over pan, and invert. Place tarte on a large plate.

Plating:

Preheat radiant oven to 375°. Slice tarte. Place desired portions on a small baking sheet, and heat until apples are hot to the touch approximately seven minutes. Center slice on dessert plate. Tuck in a scoop of vanilla bean ice cream.

Yield:

eight servings

Vanilla Bean Ice Cream

1 vanilla bean, split lengthwise

1 cup granulated sugar, divided

16 ounces whole milk

6 large egg yolks, room temperature

8 ounces heavy cream, cold

Procedure:

Place a two quart glass measure cup into a large stainless bowl, and pack bowl with ice. Place a fine sieve atop glass cup.

Scrape vanilla bean into 1/2 cup sugar, and combine. Pour milk, vanilla bean, and vanilla sugar into a two quart saucepan, and stir to combine. Bring mixture to the boil stirring frequently; cover, and remove from heat. Allow milk mixture to steep for twenty minutes.

Pour yolks into a medium-sized bowl, add remaining sugar, and whisk until thickened and pale yellow.

Uncover saucepan, place over a high flame, and bring to the boil stirring frequently. Steadily whisk milk mixture into yolks to *temper*. Pour mixture into saucepan. Place saucepan over a low flame, and stir cream constantly with a rubber spatula until it begins to thicken, and reaches 160°. Do *not* allow custard cream to boil.

Immediately pass custard cream through sieve into glass measure cup. Pour cold water over ice to speed the cooling process. Stir custard cream frequently as it cools approximately thirty minutes. Remove vanilla bean, and stir in cold heavy cream.

Pour into ice-cream freezer, and proceed with manufacturer's directions.

Yield:

one quart

temper. to incorporate a hot liquid into an egg mixture to equalize temperature

Hubbard Squash and Crystallized Ginger Tart
~myers's rum chantilly cream

Pâte Sucrée

1/4 pound unsalted butter, softened

2 3/4 ounces granulated sugar

1/8 teaspoon salt

1 large egg yolk

1/2 tablespoon light cream

1/2 teaspoon vanilla extract

1/2 lemon, zested and minced

4 1/2 ounces unbleached all purpose flour

unsalted butter, as needed

pastry flour, as needed

1 egg combined with 1 tablespoon cold water for egg wash

Hubbard Squash and Crystallized Ginger Tart

salt, as needed

1 pound Hubbard squash, peeled and seeded (weight after peeling)

1/2 cup granulated sugar

1 tablespoon molasses

1/2 teaspoon ground ginger

1/4 teaspoon freshly grated nutmeg

1/4 teaspoon cinnamon

1/8 teaspoon cloves

1 extra large egg, room temperature

1 extra large egg yolk, room temperature

7 ounces evaporated milk

1 1/2 ounce Myers's® rum

3 tablespoons crystallized ginger, thinly slivered and divided

Myers's Rum Chantilly Cream

8 ounces heavy cream

3/4 tablespoon granulated sugar

1 tablespoon Myers's® rum

1/4 teaspoon vanilla extract

Procedure for Pâte Sucrée:

Place butter, sugar, and salt into a 5-quart KitchenAid® mixer bowl, and attach flat beater; cream mixture until smooth on Stir speed. Thoroughly blend yolk, cream, vanilla extract, and lemon zest into creamed mixture. Gradually add flour, combining each addition until blended.

Scrape dough onto a sheet of plastic wrap. Use edges of plastic to gather dough. Fold plastic over dough, and flatten to a disc. Place disc inside of a plastic bag, and refrigerate dough for three hours.

Butter a 9-inch tart pan. Place unwrapped dough on a pastry-floured sheet of parchment. Dust dough with pastry flour, and cover with another sheet of parchment. Allow dough to slightly soften. Roll between parchment sheets to a 10 x 1/8-inch circle. Ease dough into tart pan, reinforce sides. Place on a baking sheet, and refrigerate for one hour.

Preheat radiant oven to 350°.

Prick bottom and sides of tart shell with a fork. Line the shell with a 10-inch circle of waxed paper, fill with beans, and place into oven. Bake until sides of shell begin to color approximately fifteen minutes. Remove waxed paper and beans, lightly brush shell with egg wash, and continue to bake until bottom appears dry approximately five minutes.

Cool tart shell completely on a rack. Do not turn off oven.

Procedure for Hubbard Squash and Crystallized Ginger Tart:

Pour approximately two inches of cold water into a two quart saucepan, and lightly season with salt. *Medium dice* squash, and arrange loosely in a steamer basket. Bring seasoned water to the boil, insert basket, and cover; steam squash until quite softened, cool briefly and purée. Pour purée into a medium-sized bowl, and cool to room temperature. Stir sugar, molasses, and spices into purée.

Whisk together egg, yolk, evaporated milk, and rum in a small bowl. Stir egg mixture thoroughly into purée. Mince 1 tablespoon of crystallized ginger, and fold evenly into filling. Pour into cooled tart shell, place on a baking sheet, and bake until filling is set approximately forty minutes.

Cool tart on a rack for twenty minutes. Carefully remove rim, and cool completely. Place tart on a flat-bottomed plate.

Procedure for Myers's Rum Chantilly Cream:

Place 5-quart KitchenAid® mixer bowl and whip into refrigerator until chilled.

Pour cream into cold bowl, and whip on medium speed until cream begins to hold shape. Add sugar, rum, and vanilla extract; continue to whip until nearly firm peak. Do *not* over whip.

Spoon Myers's® rum chantilly into a pastry bag fitted with an open-star tip, and decoratively pipe onto tart. Refrigerate until cold.

Plating:

Slice tart into desired portions. Center slice on amber glass plate. Lightly sprinkle with slivered ginger.

Yield:

ten servings

medium dice: to cut to 1/3-inch square

The Winter Season

Heavy evening clouds scent the air with moisture. Morning's light, magenta and burnt orange, illuminates a landscape rendered soft, vast, and white with newly fallen snow. Evergreens, jeweled with snowflake crystals, glisten. Meadows, fields, and marshes converge in a wonderland of silent beauty. Mountains, majestic in their robes of white, irresistibly beckon *Come play*. As faint winter sunlight fades, a pale glow of pink bathes the land.

The availability of cool weather crops is determined by favorable weather conditions. The harvesting of full-grown lobsters spawned from the North Atlantic requires icy-cold coastal waters. A heavy frost will sweeten the flavor of brussels sprouts, kale, and parsnips prior to harvest. Protected from frost—chicories, frisée, endive, radicchio, and escarole— impart a sharp and slightly bitter taste to distinctive salads. The just-picked ripeness and tart-sweet flavor of Florida's frost-free citrus fruit brighten the menu. Cool storage of cabbage, turnips, rutabaga, kohlrabi, and Jerusalem artichokes provide invigorating flavor to winter preparations.

Be warmed by the hearty rich flavors of winter.

Pork Rillettes with Sweet Onion Marmalade and Cornichon

Butter-braised sweetened onions and tart cranberries, vinegary pickles, and slightly bitter greens accompany a succulent, moist, and lightly textured pork pâté.

Bouchée of Lobster, Shrimp, and Broccoli Nantua

Creamy, rich, velvety-smooth sauce, lusciously sweet and tender shellfish, and emerald green broccoli spill from layers of buttery puff pastry.

Lemon Tartlets

Crisp, rich pastries of lemony sweet custard adorned with orange, lime, and lemon candied zest melt in your mouth.

Comforting.

ৎ
Spinach Timbales
~roasted red pepper sauce

peanut oil, as needed

4 ounces baby spinach

salt, as needed

grape seed oil, as needed

dried white bread, finely crumbled, as needed

2 pounds leaf spinach, stemmed (weight after stemming)

5 tablespoons unsalted butter, divided

1 cup Spanish onion, minced

2 cloves garlic, minced

3/4 cup Gruyère, grated

white pepper, to taste

nutmeg, freshly grated, to taste

5 large eggs, lightly beaten and room temperature

8 ounces light cream

Roasted Red Pepper Sauce (recipe follows **Spinach Timbales**)

Procedure:

Pour two inches peanut oil into a small *rondeau, and heat to 350° over a medium flame. Once temperature is reached adjust flame so temperature is maintained. Line a baking sheet with a layer of paper toweling. Carefully drop baby spinach into hot oil without crowding. Use a skimmer to constantly move leaves. Fry briefly until spinach is crisped and emerald green. Transfer with skimmer to baking sheet, lightly salt, and separate leaves.

Preheat radiant oven to 325. Lightly brush eight 6-ounce timbale molds with grape seed oil, and dust with bread crumbs. Place into a small roasting pan lined with a layer of paper towels. Fill a kettle with water, and bring to the boil.

Rinse, drain, and spin-dry leaf spinach. Heat an eight quart stockpot over a low flame; add 2 tablespoons butter and melt. Stir in onion and garlic; *sweat. Stir in spinach, lightly salt and cover. Steam for one minute or until barely wilted. Transfer into food processor work bowl fitted with metal blade; cool, and purée. Scrape mixture into a medium-sized stainless bowl. Stir in Gruyère and 1/2 cup breadcrumbs, season, and add eggs to combine. Pour cream into a small saucepan, add remaining butter, and bring to the boil. Steadily whisk into egg mixture to *temper. Pour evenly into prepared molds. Pour hot water into roasting pan to reach halfway up the sides of molds. Bake timbales until paring knife inserted into center tests clean approximately thirty minutes. Remove timbales from water, and place on a rack to rest for fifteen minutes.

Plating:

Insert a paring knife perpendicular to side of mold, and evenly encircle mold to release timbale. Gently pull timbale from edge of mold with fingertips. Invert onto the center of a rimmed glass plate, and tap bottom for full release. Create a layered petal-like design with spinach leaves on timbale, and pool plate with hot roasted red pepper sauce.

Yield:

eight servings

*sweat: to cook without color in a small amount of fat over a low flame

*temper: to incorporate a hot liquid into an egg mixture to equalize temperature

Roasted Red Pepper Sauce

12 ounces **Vegetable Stock** (see recipe for **Vegetable Stock**, page 95)

3 pounds red bell peppers

1 small jalapeño

6 small shallots, peeled

6 cloves garlic, peeled

olive oil, as needed

16 ounces dry white wine

salt, freshly ground black pepper, and cayenne, to taste

Procedure:

Preheat radiant oven to 400°.

Place red peppers, jalapeño, shallots, and garlic into a small roasting pan. Rub vegetables with oil, and place into oven. Roast for twenty minutes. Turn vegetables, and continue to roast and turn until shallots and garlic caramelize, and peppers are charred. Transfer shallots and garlic to a plate to cool. Place bell peppers and jalapeño into a small bowl; cover with plastic wrap to steam for thirty minutes. Seed and skin all peppers. Do not rinse.

Pour vegetable stock into a small saucepan, and bring to the boil. Remove from heat.

Place jalapeño, garlic, and shallots into food processor work bowl fitted with metal blade, and process briefly. Scrape into a small saucepan, stir in wine, and place over a medium-high flame; reduce until syrupy stirring frequently. Pour mixture into processor work bowl add red peppers, and purée. With food processor running, pour hot stock into puréed vegetables. Pass mixture through a Foley food mill into a two quart saucepan; discard solids.

Place saucepan over a low flame, and bring sauce to a simmer; season to taste.

Yield:

one pint

Pork Rillettes with Sweet Onion Marmalade and Cornichons

2 1/2 pounds pork butt

1 pound pork neck bones, cracked

1 1/2 quart **Chicken Stock** (see recipe for **Chicken Stock**, page 35)

1 pound Spanish onion, *medium dice*

1/2 pound carrot, *medium dice*

1/2 pound celery, *medium dice*

sachet d' épices tied in cheesecloth (3 parsley stems, 1/2 teaspoon dried thyme, 4 bay leaves, 6 whole cloves, 15 black peppercorns, and 6 cloves garlic, crushed)

salt, as needed

white pepper, as needed

rendered pork fat, warmed, as needed

frisée, rinsed and spin-dried, as needed

Sweet Onion Marmalade (recipe follows **Pork Rillettes**)

cornichons, fanned, to garnish

Procedure:

Place pork, bones, stock, onion, carrot, celery, and *sachet d' épices* into a medium-sized *rondeau*. Place over a medium flame, and bring to a low boil. Season with salt, adjust flame to low, and simmer until meat is extremely tender approximately two hours.

Strain mixture through a large sieve into a large bowl. Reserve pork, cool to room temperature, cover, and refrigerate. Press on remaining solids to release juices; discard. Fill a large bowl with ice and water. Place bowl atop ice bath until broth is cold. Refrigerate broth overnight.

Remove fat from broth, and discard. Pour into a three quart saucepan, and bring to the boil. Adjust flame to medium, and reduce volume until depth of flavor is achieved; season broth to taste.

Tear pork into medium-sized pieces; toss into KitchenAid® 5-quart mixer bowl, and attach flat beater. Turn mixer to speed 2, add hot broth and warmed pork fat as needed until taste of fat is barely apparent, and a moist, spreadable consistency is achieved; season rillettes to taste.

Pack rillettes into a one quart lidded container, cover, and refrigerate.

Plating:

Allow rillettes to stand at room temperature for twenty minutes prior to serving. Arrange frisée leaves on small plates. Place a scoop (size 16) of rillettes onto leaves, and garnish with sweet onion marmalade and cornichon fans.

Yield:

eleven servings

medium dice: to cut to 1/4-inch square

sachet d' épices: a small packet of aromatic spices

rondeau: a shallow, wide, straight-sided pot with handles

Sweet Onion Marmalade

4 medium white onions

1 1/2 ounce unsalted butter

2 ounces sun dried cranberries

grenadine, to color

Procedure:

Peel, and slice onions from root to stem; quarter onions, and very thinly slice.

Melt butter in a large skillet placed over a medium-low flame. Add onions and cranberries, and *sweat* tossing often until onions are translucent. Do *not* allow onions to brown. Add grenadine to slightly color marmalade.

Cool marmalade to room temperature; scrape into a lidded container, cover, and refrigerate.

Yield:

one (scant) pint

sweat: to cook without color in a small amount of fat over a low flame

Farfalle with Cremini, Smoked Salmon, and Green Peppercorn

6 ounces dried farfalle pasta

salt, as needed

2 ounces unsalted butter

6 tablespoons shallots, minced

6 ounces cremini mushrooms, cleaned and thinly sliced

6 ounces dry white wine

16 ounces heavy cream

2 ounces smoked salmon, sliced to 1/4-inch strips

1 1/2 teaspoon green peppercorns, drained, rinsed, and crushed

freshly ground black pepper, to taste

parsley, finely chopped, to garnish

Procedure:

Fill a six quart pasta pot with cold water, and bring to the boil; season with salt to taste the salt. Cook farfalle al dente.

While pasta is cooking, melt butter in a ten inch skillet placed over a medium-high flame until sizzling. Add shallots and mushrooms; briefly *sauté*. Add wine, and reduce until nearly evaporated stirring constantly. Whisk in cream, and reduce just until cream begins to thicken whisking occasionally. Stir in smoked salmon and peppercorns, and remove from heat.

Drain farfalle; do not rinse. Fold pasta into sauce until evenly coated, and season to taste.

Plating:

Spoon farfalle and sauce into four warmed pasta bowls placed on large plates. Sprinkle with parsley.

Yield:

four servings

sauté: to cook quickly in a small amount of fat

Pan-Roasted Quail with Cinnamon and French Lentils

Small Game Marinade

2 1/2 ounces dry white wine

1 1/2 ounce fresh lemon juice

2 large shallots, thinly sliced

4 cloves garlic, crushed

freshly ground black pepper, as needed

1 teaspoon ground cumin

1/2 teaspoon ground coriander

refined sunflower oil, as needed

4 farm-raised semi boneless quail, well rinsed and trussed

salt, as needed

4 slices cob-smoked bacon

Cinnamon and French Lentils

3/4 tablespoon cumin seed

1 cinnamon stick

1 ounce unsalted butter

5 ounces smoked ham, *small dice*

1/2 cup leek, white part only, well-rinsed and thinly sliced

1/4 cup carrot, *small dice*

1/4 cup celery, *small dice*

1 teaspoon ground cinnamon

1 cup French lentils, rinsed

14 ounces **Chicken Stock** (see recipe for **Chicken Stock**, page 35)

salt and freshly ground black pepper, to taste

4 cilantro bouquets, rinsed and dried, to garnish

Procedure for Marinating Quail:

Combine wine, lemon juice, shallots, garlic, 2 teaspoons black pepper, cumin, and coriander in a small bowl. Whisk in 10 ounces oil to emulsify. Tightly tuck quail into a small container. Pour marinade over quail, cover, and refrigerate overnight.

Procedure for Cinnamon and French Lentils:

Heat a three quart saucepan over a medium flame. Add cumin, and lightly toast until aroma is released shaking pan frequently. Add cinnamon stick, and adjust flame to low. Add butter to melt. Stir in ham, leek, carrot, and celery, and *sweat*. Stir in ground cinnamon, lentils, and stock. Bring mixture to the boil, reduce flame to low, and cover. Simmer until lentils are tender approximately twenty minutes.

Preheat radiant oven to 425°. Heat a ten inch cast-iron skillet over a medium-high flame.

Remove quail from marinade, pat dry with toweling, and season with salt and black pepper. Discard marinade.

Lightly film skillet with oil, and *sear* quail until skin is evenly golden. Remove skillet from heat, and wrap quail with bacon. Place skillet into oven, and roast for eight minutes. Remove bacon, roll quail in accumulated fat, and set breast side up in skillet. Roast until breast meat is faintly pink, and juices run clear from cavities approximately five minutes. Transfer quail to a cutting board to rest briefly.

Season lentils to taste, and discard cinnamon stick; cover, and remove from heat. Remove trussing twine from quails.

Plating:

Spoon a nest of lentils on four warmed large plates. Set quails on nests, and garnish with cilantro bouquets.

Yield:

four servings

small dice: to cut to 1/4-inch square

sweat: to cook without color in a small amount of fat over a low flame

sear: to brown the surface of food in fat over a high flame

෴

Brown Bread

2/3 cup dates, chopped

16 ounces buttermilk

unsalted butter, as needed

1 cup unbleached all purpose flour

2 cups stone ground whole wheat flour

1 teaspoon salt

2 teaspoons (scant) baking soda

6 ounces molasses

1/2 cup granulated sugar

Procedure:

Combine dates and buttermilk in a small bowl. Cover with plastic wrap, and refrigerate overnight. Strain mixture through a sieve placed over a small bowl; reserve dates and buttermilk separately.

Preheat radiant oven to 350°. Butter two 8 x 4 x 3-inch loaf pans.

Combine flours, salt, and baking soda in a medium-sized bowl.

Whisk molasses and sugar into buttermilk. Stir liquid into dry ingredients just until combined. Fold in dates.

Divide batter evenly between prepared pans, and place on a baking sheet.

Bake breads until a wooden skewer inserted into the center tests dry approximately forty-three minutes.

Place loaves on a rack to cool for ten minutes. Turn breads out onto racks, and cool completely.

Yield:

two breads

Parmesan Breadsticks

4 ounces warm water, 110°

1/4 ounce dry active yeast

1/2 teaspoon granulated sugar

2 tablespoons olive oil, and additional for oiling bowl

1/4 cup and 2 tablespoons Parmigiano Reggiano, grated and divided

2 cups unbleached all purpose flour

1 teaspoon salt

cornmeal, as needed

1 egg white combined with 1 tablespoon cold water for egg wash

Procedure:

Pour 4 ounces water into a warmed 5-quart KitchenAid® mixer bowl, sprinkle in yeast and sugar, and whisk to combine. Allow yeast to *proof* for ten minutes.

Attach dough hook to mixer. Add oil, 1/4 cup Parmigiano Reggiano, and flour, and turn mixer to speed Stir. *Knead* until dough begins to form. Add salt. Add additional flour or water as needed to achieve a moist dough. Adjust speed to 2, and *knead* for five minutes.

Turn dough out onto work surface, and continue *kneading* by hand until dough feels smooth and elastic.

Lightly oil a small bowl. Place dough into bowl, oiled side up, and cover with plastic wrap and a tea towel. Allow dough to rise in a warm area until doubled in bulk in a warm area.

Preheat radiant oven to 425°. Line a baking sheet with parchment, and dust lightly with cornmeal.

Turn dough out onto work surface, flatten, and cover with a dampened tea towel; rest dough for five minutes.

Roll dough to a 7 x 12-inch rectangle. Slice dough into twelve 7-inch strips with a pizza wheel. Gently twist each strip and place equally spaced on prepared baking sheet.

Brush strips with egg wash, and dust with remaining Parmigiano Reggiano.

Bake breadsticks for fifteen minutes, turn baking sheet, and continue to bake until evenly golden brown approximately five minutes.

Place baking sheet on a rack to cool.

To serve breadsticks preheat radiant oven to 375°. Place baking sheet into oven to warm breadsticks for five minutes.

Yield:

twelve breadsticks

proof: to allow yeast to rise

knead: to develop gluten in dough to expand and hold carbon dioxide

Pain au Lait

2 ounces unsalted butter

8 ounces whole milk

1/2 ounce dry active yeast

1/2 ounce granulated sugar

1 large egg, room temperature

1 pound bread flour

2 teaspoons salt

safflower oil, as needed

1 egg yolk combined with 1 tablespoon light cream for egg wash

Procedure:

Combine butter and milk in a small saucepan, and place over a low flame. Heat mixture until butter melts, and temperature reaches 105°. Pour into a warmed 5-quart KitchenAid® mixer bowl, and whisk in yeast and sugar. Allow yeast to *proof* for ten minutes.

Attach dough hook to mixer. Add egg and flour, and turn to speed Stir. *Knead* until dough begins to form. Add salt. Add additional flour or water as needed to achieve a moist, slightly sticky dough. Adjust to speed 2, and *knead* for five minutes.

Turn dough out onto work surface, and continue *kneading* by hand until dough feels smooth and elastic.

Lightly oil a medium-sized bowl. Place dough into bowl, oiled side up, and cover with plastic wrap and a tea towel. Allow dough to rise in a warm area until doubled in bulk.

Line a baking sheet with parchment.

Turn dough out onto work surface, and flatten. Cover with a dampened tea towel, and rest for five minutes.

Roll to *2 fold* dough. Cover with dampened tea towel, and rest for five minutes.

Scale dough into two and a half ounce portions, *round*, and place on prepared baking sheet. Cover with dampened tea towel, and rise until doubled in bulk in a warm area.

Preheat radiant oven to 375°.

Brush rolls with egg wash from bottom to top, and cut one slash into tops.

Bake for twelve minutes, turn baking sheet, and continue to bake until rolls are deeply golden brown approximately six minutes.

Cool rolls completely on a rack.

Yield:

twelve rolls

proof: to allow yeast to rise

knead: to develop gluten in dough to expand and hold carbon dioxide

2 fold: Square flattened dough. Beginning at top of the dough, fold one-half down; gently seal seam. Bring bottom of dough up and over forming a log shape, and gently seal seam.

round: to shape dough into a tight, smooth ball

Olive Loaves

10 ounces warm water, 110°

1/2 ounce dry active yeast

dash granulated sugar

2 1/2 cups bread flour

3/4 cup high-gluten flour

1 cup whole wheat flour

2 ounces Niçoise olives, pitted and chopped

2 ounces Picholine olives, pitted and chopped

2 1/4 teaspoons salt

3 tablespoons olive oil, and additional for oiling bowl

4 ounces Parmigiano Reggiano, freshly grated

cornmeal, as needed

1 egg white combined with 1 tablespoon cold water for egg wash

Procedure:

Pour 10 ounces water into a warmed 5-quart KitchenAid® mixer bowl, and whisk in yeast and sugar. Allow yeast to *proof for ten minutes.

Attach dough hook to mixer. Add bread flour, high-gluten and whole wheat flours, and olives, and begin *kneading on Stir speed until dough begins to form. Add salt, and steadily add olive oil. Add additional flour or water as needed to achieve a smooth dough, neither too moist nor too dry. Adjust to speed 2, and *knead for five minutes. Gradually add Parmigiano Reggiano, and continue to *knead for three minutes.

Turn dough out onto work surface, and *knead by hand until dough feels smooth and elastic.

Lightly oil a medium-sized bowl. Place dough into bowl, oiled side up, and cover with plastic wrap and a tea towel. Allow dough to rise in a warm area until fully doubled in bulk. Gently deflate dough with fist, re-cover, and rise again until nearly doubled.

Line a baking sheet with parchment, and dust with cornmeal.

Turn dough out onto work surface, and flatten. Cover dough with a dampened tea towel, and rest for five minutes.

Roll to *3 fold dough. Cover with dampened tea towel, and rest for five minutes.

Scale dough into two equal portions. Place portions smooth side down on work surface, and flatten. With moistened hands fold sides of portions into center, and seal forming circles; flip portions over, and *round. Place on prepared baking sheet, and cover with dampened tea towel. Allow loaves to rise until doubled in bulk.

Preheat radiant oven to 400°. Fill a cake pan with water.

Brush loaves with egg wash from bottom to top, and slash an X into tops. Place pan of water on lowest oven rack.

Place baking sheet on center oven rack, hit cake pan to create steam, and close the door.

Bake for twenty minutes, turn baking sheet, and continue to bake until deeply golden brown, and bottoms sound hollow when tapped approximately fifteen minutes. Turn off oven, and slightly open door. Allow loaves to remain in oven for five minutes to develop crust.

Cool completely on a rack.

Yield:

two loaves

*proof: to allow yeast to rise

*knead: to develop gluten in dough to expand and hold carbon dioxide

*3 fold: Square flattened dough. Beginning at top of dough, fold one-third down; gently seal seam. Repeat the fold. For the third fold, bring bottom of dough up and over forming a log shape; gently seal seam.

*round: to shape dough into a tight, smooth ball

ى

Oyster Chowder

Fish Fumet

2 1/4 pounds white fish bones

1 quart cold water

16 ounces dry white wine

1/4 pound Spanish onion, sliced

1 ounce fresh lemon juice

sachet d' épices tied in cheesecloth (3 parsley stems, 1/2 teaspoon dried thyme, 1 clove garlic, peeled, 1 bay leaf, and 3 white peppercorns)

Oyster Chowder

5 pounds live farm-raised oysters

salt, as needed

fish *fumet* (see Procedure)

2 ounces unsalted butter

4 ounces Spanish onion, *small dice*

1 leek, white part only, well-rinsed and thinly sliced

1 stalk celery, *small dice*

8 ounces heavy cream

10 ounces waxy potato, peeled and *small dice* (weight after peeling)

salt and white pepper, to taste

parsley, finely chopped, to garnish

Procedure for Fish Fumet:

Add all *fumet* ingredients into a medium-sized stainless *rondeau*, and bring to the boil. Adjust flame to low, and simmer for forty-five minutes; discard surface impurities. Do *not* stir. Strain through a sieve into a medium-sized bowl; discard solids. Rinse *rondeau*, and reserve *fumet*.

Procedure for Oyster Chowder:

Scrub oysters well under cold running water until water runs clear. Place oysters into a large bowl of cold water, and add a dash of salt. Allow to soak for one hour to release sand. Drain and rinse; discard opened oysters.

Pour *fumet* into *rondeau*, and bring to the boil; add oysters, cover, and steam until shells open. Transfer oysters into a large bowl with a slotted spoon. Sever oysters from muscle with tip of oyster knife, and remove from shells. Place into a lidded container, cover, and refrigerate. Discard unopened mussels. Strain oyster broth through a fine sieve double lined with cheesecloth into a two quart saucepan. Bring to a gentle boil over a medium-high flame, and cook briefly to develop flavor.

Wash *rondeau*, place over a low flame, and add butter to melt. Add onion, leek, and celery, and *sweat*. Pour cream into a small saucepan, and heat over a low flame. Stir oyster broth into vegetables, and bring to the boil; add potatoes, and cook until tender. Reduce flame to medium-low, whisk in cream, and cook to achieve depth of flavor and consistency. Adjust flame to low, add oysters, and simmer until heated through; season to taste.

Plating:

Ladle chowder into four warmed large bowls. Garnish with parsley.

Yield:

four servings

sachet d' épices: a small packet of aromatic spices

small dice: to cut to 1/4-inch square

fumet: a highly flavored broth of aromatic ingredients and wine

rondeau: a shallow, wide, straight-sided pot with two loop handles

sweat: to cook without color in a small amount of fat over a low flame

French Onion Soup

Remouillage

veal bones from a prepared **Veal Stock** (see recipe for **Veal Stock**, page 49)

6 ounces Spanish onion, *medium dice*

3 ounces carrot, *medium dice*

3 ounces celery, *medium dice*

sachet d' épices tied in cheesecloth (3 parsley stems, 1/2 teaspoon dried thyme, 1 clove garlic, peeled, 1 bay leaf, and 3 black peppercorns)

cold water, as needed

French Onion Soup

2 large Spanish onions

2 ounces unsalted butter

2 ounces Vermont Pomme de Vie

1/4 teaspoon freshly ground black pepper

1 quart *remouillage* (see Procedure)

salt, to taste

8 thin slices baguette

1 clove garlic, halved

8 ounces Gruyère, grated

Procedure for Remouillage:

Place bones, onion, carrot, celery, and *sachet d' épices* into a small stockpot. Add cold water to reach two inches above bones, bring to the boil, adjust flame to low, and simmer for four hours. Strain through a sieve into a large bowl; press on solids to extract juices. Discard solids.

Quickly cool *remouillage*; refrigerate overnight. Remove fat cap, and discard.

Procedure for French Onion Soup:

Peel, and slice onions from root to stem. Quarter onions, and very thinly slice. Pour 1 quart *remouillage* into a two quart saucepan, bring to the boil, and remove from heat. Freeze *remouillage* remaining for another use.

Place a medium-sized *rondeau* over a medium-low flame, add butter and melt. Add onions, and *sweat* until translucent and soft stirring occasionally. Add Pomme de Vie, adjust flame to medium-high, and caramelize onions until lightly golden scraping bottom of pan frequently. Season with 1/4 teaspoon black pepper, stir in 8 ounces *remouillage*, and bring to the boil. Adjust flame to medium-low, and gently boil for five minutes. Stir in remaining *remouillage*, bring to the boil, adjust flame to low, and simmer until depth of flavor is achieved approximately forty minutes; season lightly with salt.

Preheat broiler. Set one rack in second position from the top, and one in the middle position. Place baguette slices onto a rack-lined baking sheet, and place on middle rack. Lightly toast both sides. Check frequently to prevent burning. Place baking sheet on a cooling rack. Rub toasts with garlic on one side only. Do not turn off broiler.

Plating:

Pour an equal amount of broth and onions into four 6-ounce china ramekins, and place on a baking sheet. Float two slices of garlic toast atop broth, sprinkle with Gruyère, and place on second rack. *Gratiné* until cheese is browned and bubbly. Serve on doily-lined large plates.

Yield:

four servings

medium dice: to cut to 1/3-inch square

sachet d' épices: a small bag of aromatic spices

remouillage: a secondary stock prepared with the bones used to prepare a stock

rondeau: a shallow, wide, straight-sided pot with handles

sweat: to cook without color in a small amount of fat over a low flame

gratiné: to brown in a hot oven or under the broiler

Potato-Leek Cream with Crispy Leeks

Crispy Leeks

peanut oil, as needed

2 leeks, white and light green part, well-rinsed and dried

salt, to taste

Potato-Leek Cream

1 1/2 ounce unsalted butter

3 leeks, white and light green part, well-rinsed and thinly sliced

1 1/4 pound waxy potatoes, peeled and *small dice* (weight after peeling)

salt and white pepper, to taste

40 ounces **Chicken Stock** (see recipe for **Chicken Stock**, page 35)

8 ounces heavy cream

Procedure for Crispy Leeks:

Pour two inches of oil into a small stockpot, and heat to 350° over a medium flame. Once temperature is reached adjust flame so temperature is maintained.

Finely *julienne* leeks while oil is heating. Line a baking sheet with a layer of paper towels.

Carefully drop leeks into hot oil without crowding. Use a skimmer to constantly move leeks to prevent overbrowning. Fry leeks until lightly golden brown. Transfer with a skimmer to towel-lined baking sheet; lightly season with salt. Separate leeks, and reserve.

Strain oil through a cheesecloth-lined sieve into a glass jar. Cool, cover, and store away from light for another use.

Procedure for Potato-Leek Cream:

Heat a medium-sized stainless *rondeau* over a low flame, add butter and melt. Add leeks, and *sweat*. Stir in potato, and evenly coat with buttered leeks. Lightly season vegetables; stir in stock, and bring to the boil. Adjust flame to low, and simmer until potatoes are tender stirring frequently. Skim and discard impurities from the surface.

Pour cream into a small saucepan, and heat over a low flame.

Strain vegetable mixture through a sieve placed over a medium-sized bowl; reserve stock and vegetables separately. Purée vegetables until very smooth adding liquid as needed. Rinse *rondeau*, and pour in purée. Steadily whisk in remaining liquid to fully incorporate. Place over a low flame, whisk in cream, and simmer until consistency and depth of flavor is achieved; season to taste.

Plating:

Ladle potato-leek cream into warmed deep bowls. Place a nest of crispy leeks in the center of each bowl to garnish.

Yield:

six servings

small dice: to cut to 1/4-inch square

julienne: to thinly slice to long, thin 1/8-inch rectangular strips

rondeau: a shallow, wide, straight-sided pot with handles

sweat: to cook without color in a small amount of fat over a low flame

Cream of Cauliflower Soup

6 cups small cauliflower florets, divided

salt, as needed

4 slices cob-smoked bacon

2 ounces unsalted butter

2 leeks, white part only, well-rinsed and thinly sliced

1 stalk celery, *small dice*

1 teaspoon garlic, minced

1 quart **Chicken Stock** (see recipe for **Chicken Stock**, page 35)

1 bay leaf

8 ounces heavy cream

dash nutmeg, freshly grated

white pepper, to taste

3 ounces Vermont medium orange cheddar, shredded

Procedure:

Fill a small bowl with ice and water. Pour two inches cold water into a two quart saucepan, season with salt, and bring to the boil. Arrange 2 cups cauliflower florets loosely in a steamer basket, set into saucepan, cover and *blanch* until florets are tender. *Shock* in ice bath, and drain well. Place in small bowl, and refrigerate.

Half fill a small saucepan with cold water, and bring to the boil; add bacon, and *blanch* until water begins to boil. Drain, rinse with cold water, and pat dry. Chop bacon. Toss into a small *rondeau*, and place over a low flame. Cook until fat is rendered, and bacon is crisped. Transfer bacon to a paper towel-lined plate, and reserve. Stir butter into rendered fat. Add remaining cauliflower, leeks, celery, and garlic; *sweat* stirring occasionally. Stir in stock and bay leaf. Bring to the boil, adjust flame to low, and simmer vegetable mixture for twenty minutes.

Pour heavy cream into a small saucepan. Place over a medium flame, and reduce volume by half whisking frequently.

Strain vegetable mixture through a sieve placed over a medium-sized bowl; discard bay leaf, and reserve liquid and vegetables separately. Purée vegetables until very smooth adding liquid as needed. Pour purée into rinsed *rondeau*. Steadily whisk in liquid to fully incorporate, and place over a low flame. Whisk in cream, stir in florets, season and heat through.

Plating:

Ladle soup into warmed bowls. Garnish with cheddar and bacon.

Yield:

four servings

small dice: to cut to 1/4-inch square

blanch: to cook briefly in boiling water or hot fat

shock: to stop the cooking process

rondeau: a shallow, wide, straight-sided pot with handles

sweat: to cook without color in a small amount of fat over a low flame

ᔰ

Bosc Pear with Vermont Blue and Bitter Greens
~balsamic vinaigrette

Balsamic Vinaigrette

1 1/2 ounce balsamic vinegar

1 1/2 ounce dry white wine

2 teaspoons shallots, minced

1/4 teaspoon Coleman's® dry mustard

1 2/3 ounce walnut oil

3 ounces safflower oil

granulated sugar and salt, to taste

Salad

2 ripe Bosc pears

Gia Russa Balsamic Glaze®, as needed

2 ounces Vermont blue cheese, crumbled

2 ounces loose-leaf chicory, rinsed, spin-dried, and torn bite-sized

1 ounce radicchio, *chiffonade*

2 ounces walnuts, lightly toasted and chopped, to garnish

Procedure for Balsamic Vinaigrette:

Pour vinegar, wine, shallots, and dry mustard into food processor work bowl fitted with metal blade; process until blended. Combine both oils. With motor running, slowly add oil to emulsify; season lightly with sugar and salt. Pour vinaigrette into a lidded jar, cover, and refrigerate.

Procedure for Salad:

Cut pears in half lengthwise; remove core with a melon scoop, and slice tough stem from flesh. Evenly brush cut surface of pears with balsamic glaze, and mound cavities with small pieces of cheese.

Plating:

Combine greens, and mound on four chilled glass plates. Drizzle vinaigrette over greens. Center cheese-filled pears, and scatter plates with walnuts to garnish.

Yield:

four servings

chiffonade: to finely julienne

Citrus Salad

Salad

1 pink grapefruit

1 blood orange

1 clementine

2 ounces daikon radish, peeled and *small dice*

1 ounce jícama, peeled and *small dice*

1/2 ounce red onion, *small dice*

1 teaspoon lime zest, minced

4 ounces iceberg lettuce, rinsed, spin-dried, and *chiffonade*

2 ounces radicchio, *chiffonade*

salt and freshly ground black pepper, to taste

Citrus Vinaigrette

1 1/2 ounce citrus juice (see Procedure)

2 teaspoons fresh lime juice

1/4 teaspoon honey

1/4 teaspoon New Mexico red chile powder

1/4 teaspoon freshly ground black pepper

3 ounces safflower oil

salt, to taste

Procedure for Citrus Salad:

Remove peel and white pith from citrus fruit. Slice off stem end of each fruit and place cut side down on work surface. Set a sharp, flexible knife at a 45°angle to fruit. Slice fruit in sections from top to bottom remove both peel and white pith with each slice.

Remove fruit segments by holding fruit in one hand over a small bowl. Set knife perpendicular to fruit. Slice in between the membrane of each segment allowing fruit and juices to collect in bowl. Strain through a sieve placed over an eight ounce glass measure cup. Pour fruit back into bowl; reserve juices for vinaigrette. Combine daikon radish, jícama, onion, and zest with citrus fruit.

Procedure for Citrus Vinaigrette:

Pour 1 1/2 ounce citrus juice, lime juice, honey, chile powder, and black pepper into food processor work bowl fitted with metal blade; process until blended.

With machine running, slowly add oil to emulsify; lightly season with salt.

Plating:

Combine iceberg and radicchio. Season, and dress greens lightly with vinaigrette; toss to coat. Pile greens high on four chilled plates, and mound with citrus salad.

Yield:

four servings

*small dice: to cut to 1/4-inch square

*chiffonade: to finely julienne

Salad of Escarole, Endive, and Garlic Croutons
~warm red wine-mustard vinaigrette

5 ounces tender escarole, rinsed, spin-dried, and torn bite-sized

2 ounces Belgium endive, thinly sliced

1 1/2 ounce extra virgin olive oil, divided

1 1/2 ounce refined sunflower oil

1 small shallot, minced

freshly ground black pepper, as needed

1 ounce oak aged red wine vinegar

3/4 tablespoon Grey Poupon® Dijon mustard

salt, to taste

Garlic Croutons, as needed (see recipe for **Garlic Croutons,** page104)

Procedure:

Combine greens in a large bowl, cover with a dampened tea towel, and refrigerate.

Combine oils. Heat 1 ounce oil in a small sauté pan placed over a low flame. Add shallot, season with black pepper, and *sweat*. Whisk in vinegar to combine. Steadily whisk in remaining oil, season lightly with salt, and remove from heat. Whisk in mustard to emulsify.

Pour warm vinaigrette over greens, season, and toss to evenly coat. Scatter croutons, and toss lightly.

Plating:

Arrange salad on square plates, and serve.

Yield:

four servings

sweat. to cook without color in a small amount of fat over a low flame

White Bean and Chorizo Salad

White Beans

1/2 cup dried navy beans

1 quart cold water

1/2 small Spanish onion

1 jalapeño

sachet d' épices tied in cheesecloth (3 parsley stems, 1/2 teaspoon dried thyme, 1 clove garlic, peeled, 1bay leaf, and 3 black peppercorns)

6 ounces chorizo sausage

Garlic Vinaigrette

2 medium cloves garlic, chopped

1 1/8 ounce champagne vinegar

3/4 ounce cold water

3/4 teaspoon Grey Poupon® Dijon mustard

freshly ground black pepper, as needed

2 1/2 ounces olive oil

1 1/4 ounce safflower oil

salt, to taste

Salad

2 stalks celery, peeled and *small dice*

1 carrot, *small dice*

4 tablespoons red onion, *small dice*

1 tablespoon chipotle chile in adobo sauce, minced

2 tablespoons pimento, *small dice*

2 tablespoons cilantro, rinsed, spin-dried and chopped

salt and freshly ground black pepper, to taste

12 green chicory leaves, rinsed, dried and trimmed

Procedure for White Beans:

Wash and pick over beans. Pour into a medium-sized bowl, add cold water to cover, and wrap bowl with plastic. Soak beans overnight. Drain; pour into a two quart saucepan, add onion, jalapeño, and *sachet d' épices,* and cover with cold water by three inches. Bring to the boil, and adjust flame to low; simmer beans for fifteen minutes. Add chorizo, and simmer for twenty minutes; remove chorizo, cool, and *small dice.* Taste beans; simmer as needed until tender. Allow beans to cool to room temperature. Strain through a sieve placed over a medium-sized bowl. Discard seasoning vegetables. Pour beans into a small bowl. Cool broth; pour into a lidded container, cover, and freeze for another use.

Procedure for Garlic Vinaigrette:

Mince garlic in food processor work bowl fitted with metal blade; add vinegar, water, and Dijon, season with black pepper, and process to combine. Combine oils. With machine running, steadily add oil to emulsify; season lightly.

Procedure for Salad:

Fold chorizo, celery, carrot, onion, chipotle chile, pimento, and cilantro into beans; season to taste. Dress salad with vinaigrette, cover bowl with plastic wrap, and refrigerate for one hour.

Plating:

Spiral chicory leaves on large plates, and mound salad in center of leaves.

Yield:

six servings

small dice: to cut to1/4-inch square

sachet d' épices: a small packet of aromatic spices

ల

Osso Bucco

2, 2-pound hind veal shanks, crosscut

salt and freshly ground black pepper, as needed

3 ounces unbleached all purpose flour

olive oil, as needed

2 medium Spanish onions, halved and thinly sliced

2 large carrots, thinly sliced

3 cloves garlic, minced

4 ounces soft red wine

3/4 cup quality canned plum tomatoes and juices, chopped

5 to 6 cups **Veal Stock** (see recipe for **Veal Stock**, page 49)

1 bay leaf

2 teaspoons lemon zest, minced

1 Roma tomato, seeded and *small dice*

Parmesan and Gruyère Whipped Potatoes

(see recipe for **Parmesan and Gruyère Whipped Potatoes**, page 114)

1 tablespoon parsley, finely chopped

1 teaspoon tarragon, chopped

Procedure:

Season veal, and pour flour into a pie tin. Lightly dredge veal; shake off excess. Discard unused flour.

Place a large *rondeau* over a medium flame; film generously with oil, and heat.

Sear shanks until golden brown on both sides. Adjust flame as needed to prevent burning; transfer shanks into a small bowl. Add additional oil as needed; stir in onions and carrots, adjust flame to medium-low, and lightly caramelize vegetables stirring occasionally. Add garlic; cook briefly.

Adjust flame to high; add wine, and reduce to a syrupy consistency stirring constantly. Add plum tomatoes and juices, veal shanks and juices, enough stock to just cover shanks, and bay leaf; bring to the boil. Adjust flame to low. Partially cover *rondeau*, and *braise* until veal is fork tender approximately one and one-half hour. Skim and discard surface impurities. Add stock as needed to nearly cover shanks. Remove shanks, and reserve.

Allow enriched stock to cool slightly; discard bay leaf, and purée. Pour into *rondeau*, and place over a low flame. Adjust consistency with cold water as needed. Stir in shanks, lemon zest, and tomato, season to taste, and heat through.

Plating:

Mound parmesan and gruyère whipped potatoes into four warmed deep bowls. Lean shanks against potatoes, and ladle generously with sauce. Sprinkle with herbs.

Yield:

four servings

small dice: to cut to 1/4-inch square

rondeau: a shallow, wide, straight-sided pot with handles

sear: to brown the surface of food in fat over a high flame

braise: to simmer partially covered in stock or another liquid

Bouchée of Lobster, Shrimp, and Broccoli Nantua

Bouchée

2.2 pounds frozen puff pastry sheets

pastry flour, as needed

1 egg combined with 1 tablespoon water for egg wash

Lobster, Shrimp, and Broccoli Nantua

4, 4-ounce raw Maine lobster tails

16, 16/20 raw shrimp, presplit and cleaned

olive oil, as needed

4 tablespoons shallots, minced

2 teaspoons sweet Hungarian paprika

36 ounces dry white wine, divided

3 1/2 quarts cold water, divided

1 large Spanish onion, *small dice*

2 small bay leaves

6 sprigs parsley

1 1/2 tablespoon black peppercorns

5 ounces heavy cream

1 ounce unsalted butter

1 1/2 ounce unbleached all purpose flour

1/4 teaspoon tomato paste

1 ounce dry sherry

6 ounces broccoli florets

salt, as needed

2 tablespoons and 2 teaspoons Better than Bouillon® lobster base

parsley, finely chopped, to garnish

Procedure for Bouchées:

Place pastry sheets on flour dusted parchment to defrost according to manufacturer's directions, and unfold. Dust pastry with flour, and roll gently one way only to a 10-inch rectangle.

Line a baking sheet with parchment. Using a china saucer as a template, cut out eight 5-inch pastry circles with tip of paring knife, and place on baking sheet.

Press a 3-inch round biscuit cutter halfway through four pastry circles to form a 2-inch ring. Lightly egg wash ring portion only of pastries, and place them washed side down onto four uncut circles. Lightly brush top ring portions only with egg wash. Cover bouchées with a sheet of parchment, and refrigerate for one hour. Freeze leftover pastry for another use.

Preheat radiant oven to 400°. Place baking sheet into oven without removing parchment. Bake for twenty-two minutes until fully risen and golden brown. Do not turn off oven.

Cool briefly on a rack. Carefully cut out centers of bouchées, and reserve; remove any uncooked pastry from interior, and discard. Place bouchées into oven for three or four minutes to dry interiors.

Cool completely on a rack.

Procedure for Lobster, Shrimp, and Broccoli Nantua:

Place lobster tails shell side down on work surface. Gently separate the flesh from shell with a sharp paring knife leaving tail flesh intact; reserve shells. Peel shrimp, and reserve shells. Cover, and refrigerate shellfish; roughly chop lobster shells, and combine with shrimp shells.

Place a small stockpot over a low flame, film with oil, and heat. Add shallots and paprika; briefly *sweat*. Adjust flame to medium-high and add shells; cook until lobster shells are a deep red color stirring constantly. Stir in 4 ounces wine, and reduce until syrupy. Pour in 1 1/2 quart cold water, remaining wine, onion, bay leaves, parsley, and peppercorns. Bring mixture to the boil, reduce flame to low, and simmer for forty-five minutes. Strain broth through a sieve into a small stainless *rondeau*; discard solids, and place over a medium-low flame to barely simmer broth.

Fill a medium-sized bowl with ice and cold water.

Poach shellfish in barely simmering broth in batches just until done. Use a skimmer to transfer into ice bath to *shock*; immediately drain shellfish. Slice lobster tails to 1 1/2-inch medallions. Combine shrimp and lobster, and refrigerate.

Pour cream into a small saucepan, and place over a low flame.

Strain broth through a cheesecloth-lined sieve into a medium-sized bowl. Place *rondeau* over a medium-low flame, add 1 ounce butter and melt. Gradually stir in flour, and cook *roux* to a pale blond color stirring constantly. Adjust flame to low and steadily whisk in broth, thoroughly incorporate each addition to prevent lumping. Simmer for twenty minutes whisking occasionally. Pour sauce through a fine sieve into medium-sized bowl. Whisk in cream, tomato paste, and sherry; cover bowl with plastic wrap.

Half fill a three quart saucepan with hot water, and bring to a simmer over a low flame. Place bowl of nantua sauce over saucepan to hold warm.

Wash *rondeau*. Pour in remaining 2 quarts cold water, and bring to the boil. Stir in lobster base; adjust flame to very low.

Pour two inches of cold water into a three quart saucepan, season with salt to taste the salt, and bring to the boil.

Place shellfish into an insert basket, and immerse basket into lobster broth.

Arrange broccoli loosely in a steamer basket; set into saucepan, cover, and steam until florets are emerald green and crisp to the bite.

Fold shellfish and broccoli into nantua sauce.

Plating:

Center bouchées on four large warmed plates. Generously fill with nantua mixture to spill over sides, sprinkle with parsley, and offset pastry centers.

Yield:

four servings

small dice: to cut to 1/4-inch square

sweat: to cook without color in a small amount of fat over a low flame

rondeau: a shallow, wide, straight-sided pot with loop handles

shock: to stop the cooking process

roux: a cooked mixture of butter and flour used to thicken liquids

Rabbit Blanquette
~straw and hay tagliatelle

Rabbit Stock

4 pounds bones from farm-raised rabbits

1 medium Spanish onion, *medium dice*

1 stalk celery, *medium dice*

1 small carrot, *medium dice*

sachet d' épices tied in cheesecloth (3 stems parsley, 1/2 teaspoon dried thyme, 1 clove garlic, peeled, 1 bay leaf, and 3 black peppercorns)

Rabbit Blanquette with Straw and Hay Tagliatelle

unsalted butter, as needed

2 ounces shallots, minced

10 ounces button mushrooms, cleaned, trimmed and quartered

6 ounces pearl onions, cooked

4 ounces fresh lemon juice

4 ounces cold water

3 pounds farm-raised rabbit stew meat, 1 1/2-inch cubed

2 ounces unbleached all purpose flour

4 ounces plain tagliatelle pasta (fettuccine may be substituted)

4 ounces spinach tagliatelle pasta (fettuccine may be substituted)

salt, as needed

1 large egg yolk

4 ounces heavy cream

white pepper, to taste

parsley, finely chopped, to garnish

Procedure for Rabbit Stock:

Rinse bones, and place into a small stockpot. Add cold water to cover bones by two inches. Bring to the boil, and adjust flame to low; skim and discard surface impurities. Add vegetables and *sachet d' épices*, and simmer stock for four hours. Strain stock through a large sieve into a medium-sized bowl. Press on solids to extract all liquid; discard solids.

Quickly cool stock; refrigerate overnight. Remove all visible fat from stock, and pour into a medium-sized *rondeau*.

Procedure for Rabbit Blanquette with Straw and Hay Tagliatelle:

Film a ten inch skillet with butter, and scatter with shallots. Add mushrooms, onions, lemon juice, and 4 ounces water.

Butter a 10-inch parchment circle, and place buttered side down on mushroom and onion mixture. Bring to the boil; adjust flame to low, and simmer until vegetables are tender approximately ten minutes. Strain through a sieve paced over a small bowl. Cool broth; pour into a lidded container, cover, and freeze for another use. Pour vegetables into bowl, and cover with parchment circle.

Place rabbit into a small stainless *rondeau*, cover with cold water, and bring to the boil. Drain rabbit, and rinse with cold water; drain thoroughly. Pour rabbit into stock, bring to the boil, and immediately adjust flame to low. Simmer rabbit until fork tender approximately one and one-half hour.

Strain enriched stock through a sieve into a large glass measure cup. Pour rabbit into a small bowl. Pour stock into a two quart saucepan, and place over a medium-high flame. Reduce stock volume to one quart, and remove from heat. Cool rabbit; cover, and reserve.

Wash *rondeau*, and place over a low flame, add 1 1/2 ounce butter and melt. Gradually stir in flour, and incorporate well. Cook *roux* to a pale blond color stirring frequently. Steadily whisk in hot stock, incorporate each addition fully to prevent lumping. Bring *velouté* to the boil; adjust flame to low, and simmer for thirty minutes stirring occasionally. Strain through a fine sieve into a medium-sized bowl. Rinse and dry *rondeau*, and pour in *velouté*.

Three-fourths fill a six quart pasta pot three-fourths full with cold water; season with salt to taste the salt, and bring to the boil.

Combine yolk and heavy cream in a small bowl. Whisk 1 cup of *velouté* into *liaison* to *temper*. Whisk all of *liaison* into remaining *velouté*. Barely simmer sauce over a very low flame for ten minutes stirring frequently. Do *not* allow sauce to boil.

Cook pasta al dente. Drain, do not rinse; season with butter, salt, and white pepper.

Stir rabbit and mushroom and onion mixture and collected juices into sauce, and season to taste; heat through.

Plating:

Create mounds by twirling pasta with tongs into the center of four deep bowls. Encircle pasta with rabbit blanquette. Sprinkle with parsley.

Yield:

four servings

medium dice: to cut to 1/3-inch square

sachet d' épices: a small packet of aromatic spices

rondeau: a shallow, wide, straight-sided pot with two loop handles

braise: to simmer partially covered in stock or another liquid

roux: a mixture of flour and butter used to thicken liquids

velouté: a sauce of white stock thickened with white roux

liaison: egg yolk and heavy cream combined to enrich sauces and soups

temper: to incorporate a hot liquid into an egg mixture to equalize temperature

Roast Tenderloin of Beef with Sauce au Poivre
~potato dauphinoise

3 pounds beef tenderloin, cleaned and trimmed

1 clove garlic, halved

olive oil, as needed

freshly ground black pepper, as needed

dried thyme, as needed

salt, as needed

6 ounces heavy cream

2 ounces unsalted butter, cold and divided

2 tablespoons shallots, minced

1 teaspoon garlic, minced

2 teaspoons pink peppercorns

2 teaspoons green peppercorns, crushed

1/2 tablespoon black peppercorns, crushed

2 ounces brandy

12 ounces **Veal Stock** (see recipe for **Veal Stock**, page 49)

Potato Dauphinoise (recipe follows **Roast Tenderloin of Beef**)

parsley, finely chopped, to garnish

Procedure for Roast Tenderloin:

Rub tenderloin with cut side of garlic, and rub lightly with oil; season with black pepper and thyme. Allow beef to stand at room temperature for thirty minutes. Preheat radiant oven to 400°. Heat a ten inch cast-iron skillet over a medium-high flame and film lightly with oil. Season tenderloin with salt, and *sear until evenly browned. Transfer tenderloin to a rack-lined roasting pan, and place skillet on stove. Roast to an internal temperature of 120° for medium-rare. Transfer to a baking sheet, and tent lightly with foil.

Procedure for Sauce au Poivre:

Pour cream into a small saucepan, and place over a low flame.

Place skillet over a low flame, add 1 ounce butter and melt. Stir in shallots, garlic, and all peppercorns, and *sweat briefly. Adjust flame to medium-high, add brandy and *flambé. When flames extinguish reduce until syrupy stirring constantly. Whisk in stock and accumulated beef juices, bring to the boil, and adjust flame to medium. Skim and discard surface impurities, and reduce to a thin sauce consistency. Whisk in cream. Cook to develop consistency and depth of flavor whisking occasionally. Season lightly, and remove from heat. Whisk in remaining butter.

Transfer tenderloin to a cutting board, and slice evenly into twelve slices.

Plating:

Place a diamond-shaped portion of potato dauphinoise at the top of four large warmed plates, and arrange overlapping slices of tenderloin at the bottom. Ladle beef with sauce, and garnish with parsley.

Yield:

four servings

*sear: to brown the surface of food in fat over a high flame

*sweat: to cook without color in a small amount of fat over a low flame

*flambé: to pour spirits over food and ignite

Potato Dauphinoise

unsalted butter, as needed

3, 10-ounce russet potatoes

2 1/2 teaspoons garlic, minced

1 1/2 tablespoon thyme leaves, chopped

3 ounces Gruyère, grated

16 ounces heavy cream

dash nutmeg, freshly grated

salt and white pepper, to taste

1 tablespoon Parmigiano Reggiano, grated

Procedure:

Preheat radiant oven to 325°. Generously butter an 8 x 8 x 2-inch glass baking dish.

Peel potatoes. Thinly slice potatoes into a medium-sized bowl using a *mandoline*. Add garlic, thyme, and Gruyère, and toss to combine.

Pour heavy cream into a one quart saucepan, place over a high flame, and bring to a scald. Pour cream over potato mixture, and toss to combine; add nutmeg and season lightly. Press potato mixture into prepared dish, and sprinkle with Parmigiano Reggiano.

Bake until potatoes are very tender approximately seventy minutes.

Allow potato dauphinoise to set for ten minutes. Slice into four diamond-shaped portions.

Yield:

four servings

mandoline: a stainless slicer with blades adjustable for cut and thickness

༄

Crème Brûlée

Custard

16 ounces heavy cream

4 large egg yolks

3 ounces granulated sugar

dash salt

1/2 vanilla bean

Sugar Glaze

1/4 pound dark brown sugar

granulated sugar, as needed

Procedure for Custard:

Preheat radiant oven to 315°. Place oven rack in third lowest position. Fill a kettle with water, and bring to the boil.

Line a shallow roasting pan with a layer of paper towels, and set six 6-ounce crème brûlée molds inside.

Pour cream into a one quart saucepan, and place over a medium-low flame stirring occasionally until warmed.

Pour yolks and sugar into a medium-sized bowl, and whisk until thickened and pale yellow. Whisk in salt and scraped soft interior of vanilla bean. Place pod inside of your sugar jar for flavor if desired, or discard. Steadily whisk warmed cream into yolk mixture without aerating.

Pour mixture through a fine sieve into a quart glass measure cup, and distribute evenly between molds. Carefully pour boiled water into roasting pan to reach halfway up the sides of molds, and place on third lowest oven rack.

Bake crèmes until set approximately forty-five minutes. Remove crèmes from water bath to a rack, and cool completely. Wrap molds with plastic wrap, and refrigerate overnight.

Procedure for Sugar Glaze:

Preheat radiant oven to 325°. Put on a pair of latex or plastic gloves.

Pour an even layer of brown sugar onto a baking sheet, and place into oven on middle shelf.

Bake sugar until moisture evaporates, and sugar feels dry. Move sugar frequently with gloved fingers to distribute heat.

Press hot, dry sugar through a sieve into a small container, *twice*. Weigh brown sugar powder, and pour into container. Weigh an equal amount of granulated sugar, and combine with powder. Pour through sieve into container. Tightly cover, and store at room temperature.

Plating:

Cover the surface of cold crème with a thin layer of sugar glaze; tap excess into container. Lightly caramelize glaze with a hand held butane torch. Repeat the procedure three times to form a thin hard crust. Place crème brûlée on a doily-lined glass plate.

Yield:

six crème brûlée

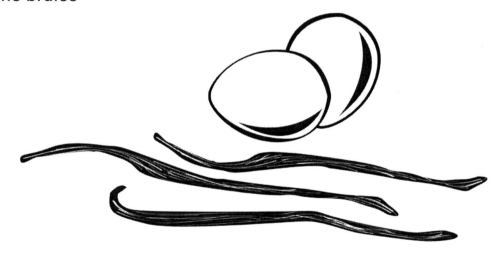

Caramelized Almond and Pear Cheesecake

Poached Pears

1 1/4 cup granulated sugar

8 ounces cold water

24 ounces dry Riesling wine

1/2 lemon, juiced

2 1/2-inch strip orange zest

1/2 stick cinnamon

3 Bosc pears, ripened

Graham Cracker Crust

8 ounces graham cracker crumbs

6 ounces granulated sugar

3 ounces unsalted butter, melted

pan spray, as needed

Caramelized Almonds

4 tablespoons granulated sugar

1/2 cup sliced almonds

Cheesecake

1 1/2 pound cream cheese, room temperature

1/2 pound granulated sugar

1/2 pound sour cream

4 large eggs, room temperature

2 large egg yolks, room temperature

1/2 tablespoon lemon zest, minced

3/4 teaspoon almond extract

1/2 tablespoon vanilla extract

1 1/4 ounce cornstarch, sifted

Procedure for Poached Pears:

Combine sugar, water, wine, lemon juice, orange zest, and cinnamon stick in a three quart saucepan, and bring to the boil. Strain syrup into a medium-sized bowl, and cool to room temperature.

Half fill a large bowl with ice and water.

Peel, halve, and core pears, and slice tough stems from flesh. Place pears onto the bottom of three quart saucepan, and cover completely with cooled syrup. Place a circle of parchment and a pan lid into saucepan to keep pears submerged. Bring mixture to a full boil, and remove from heat. Place pears into a medium-sized bowl using a skimmer, and set atop ice bath. Pour syrup over pears, and cover with parchment circle. Cool pears completely.

Procedure for Graham Cracker Crust:

Combine crumbs and sugar in a medium-sized bowl. Add melted butter, and mix until ingredients ball together when squeezed.

Preheat radiant oven to 350°. Place oven rack in third lowest position.

Lightly pan spray the bottom of an 8 x 3-inch cake pan. Place an 8-inch parchment circle onto bottom, and lightly spray parchment and sides of pan. Press a thin layer of crust mixture onto sides of pan to reach three-fourths up from bottom. Form a thin bottom layer. Press fingertips where bottom meets the sides of pan, ensuring a thin seal.

Place pan on a baking sheet, and bake crust for ten minutes. Cool crust completely on a rack. Do not turn off oven.

Procedure for Caramelized Almonds:

Line a baking sheet with parchment.

Pour sugar into a cold ten inch sauté pan, and scatter with almonds. Set pan over a high flame. As soon as sugar begins to melt shake pan constantly until almonds are lightly caramelized. Immediately pour almonds onto prepared baking sheet, and separate with a wooden spoon. Cool caramelized almonds completely.

Procedure for Cheesecake:

Lift pears from syrup with a skimmer onto a paper towel-lined plate. Pat pears lightly with a paper towel. Pour syrup through a sieve into a lidded jar, cover, and refrigerate for another use.

Place pears concentrically onto cooled crust with stem ends positioned toward center of crust.

Place cream cheese into a 5-quart KitchenAid® mixer bowl, and attach flat beater. Blend on Stir speed until cheese is very smooth. With mixer running gradually add sugar, incorporate each addition. Add sour cream, and combine well. Turn off mixer to scrape down bowl and beater.

Combine eggs, yolks, zest, and extracts. With mixer running on speed Stir gradually add egg mixture, fully incorporate each addition. Add sifted cornstarch, and blend just until incorporated.

Pour batter into pear-lined crust. Line a 12 x 10 x 6-inch hotel pan with a layer of paper towels, and set cheesecake into pan. Carefully pour hot water into hotel pan to reach halfway up the sides of cheesecake pan. Place hotel pan on third lowest oven rack, and cover with a baking sheet. Bake cheesecake for one hour. Remove baking sheet, and scatter surface with caramelized almonds. Continue to bake, uncovered, for approximately forty minutes, or until cheesecake slightly wobbles and top has domed.

Remove cheesecake from water, and place on a rack to cool completely. Wrap pan with plastic, and refrigerate overnight.

Place cheesecake over a medium-high flame and spin constantly until pan is warm to the touch; remove from heat. Insert an offset spatula perpendicular to side of pan, and evenly encircle pan to release cheesecake. Place a 9-inch cake circle over pan, and invert. Carefully remove pan and parchment. Place another cake circle onto cheesecake, and re-invert.

Plating:

Slice cheesecake into desired portions using a hot, dry, thin knife. Center slice on an amber glass plate.

Yield:

ten servings

Lemon Tartlets

Tartlets

1 recipe **Pâte Brisée** rolled to 1/8-inch thickness, and refrigerated

(see recipe for **Pâte Brisée**, page 24)

unsalted butter, as needed

pastry flour, as needed

1 egg combined with 1 tablespoon cold water for egg wash

Lemon Curd

8 ounces fresh lemon juice

dash salt

2 cups granulated sugar

8 ounces unsalted butter, cold and *medium dice*

4 extra large eggs

2 extra large egg yolks

Candied Zest

1 lemon

1 lime

1 orange

6 ounces fresh orange juice

4 ounces cold water

8 ounces granulated sugar

1 teaspoon fresh lemon juice

Procedure for Tartlets:

Butter six 4 1/2-inch tartlet pans. Place rolled pâte brisée on a lightly floured work surface. Cut out six 5 1/2-inch rounds from dough, and gently form into prepared pans, reinforce sides. Place tartlet shells on a baking sheet, and refrigerate for thirty minutes.

Preheat radiant oven to 375°. Prick sides and bottoms of shells with a fork. Line each tartlet shell with a 6-inch circle of waxed paper, and fill with beans.

Bake shells for twenty minutes, and remove from oven. Remove waxed paper and beans, and brush lightly with egg wash. Place baking sheet into oven, and bake shells briefly until golden brown.

Cool shells completely on a rack. Remove rims and bottoms of tartlet pans.

Procedure for Lemon Curd:

Pour lemon juice into a heavy-bottomed two quart saucepan, add salt, and bring to the boil. Adjust flame to low; add sugar, and stir until dissolved. Gradually stir in butter, incorporate each addition. Adjust flame to medium-high, and bring to the boil stirring constantly.

Combine eggs and yolks in a small bowl. Remove saucepan from heat. Quickly whisk 1 cup of lemon mixture into eggs to *temper*; whisk into remaining lemon mixture. Place saucepan over a medium-high flame, and whisk curd constantly until center boils. Strain through a fine sieve into a small bowl. Press plastic wrap onto surface, and cool curd to room temperature. Fill tartlet shells, smooth surface, and refrigerate until cold.

Procedure for Candied Zest:

Remove long strips of the thin, brightly colored part of the citrus rind with a sharp paring knife. Finely *julienne* zest, and place into a small sieve. Half fill a two quart saucepan with water, and bring to the boil; immerse sieve with zest, and *blanch* for thirty seconds. Immediately place sieve under cold running water; drain zest.

Combine orange juice, cold water, sugar, and lemon juice in a small saucepan, and bring to the boil. Remove from heat, and stir in zest. Cool, and pour into a lidded jar, cover, and refrigerate until cold.

Strain candied zest over a bowl; drain thoroughly, and reserve syrup.

Plating:

Center each lemon tartlet on a colorful plate. Gather an ample pinch of candied zest with fingertips, and place onto center of tartlets.

Combine remaining zest with syrup, pour into lidded jar, and refrigerate for another use.

Yield:

six tartlets

medium dice: to cut to 1/3-inch square

temper: to incorporate a hot liquid into an egg mixture to equalize temperature

julienne: to thinly slice to long, thin 1/8-inch rectangular strips

blanch: to cook briefly in boiling water or hot fat

Mocha Crèmes

grapeseed oil, as needed

3 ounces Callebaut® semisweet chocolate, chopped

3 large eggs, room temperature

6 large egg yolks, room temperature

120 grams granulated sugar

1 liter half-and-half

1/2 ounce (hefty) chocolate-flavored ground coffee

1 teaspoon vanilla extract

1 1/2 ounce Tia Maria® liquor

Chantilly Cream, to garnish (see recipe for **Chantilly Cream**, page 122)

sweet chocolate curls, to garnish

Procedure:

Preheat radiant oven to 325°. Fill a kettle with water, and bring to the boil.

Line a small shallow roasting pan with a layer of paper towels. Brush seven 6-ounce glass ramekins very lightly with oil, and set ramekins into roasting pan. Tear small slits into a sheet of aluminum foil sized to cover the roasting pan.

Half fill a three quart saucepan with water, and bring to a simmer over a low flame. Pour chocolate into a flat-bottomed medium-sized bowl, and place over simmering water stirring occasionally until melted. Turn off flame.

Pour eggs, yolks, and sugar into a medium-sized bowl, and whisk until thickened and pale yellow.

Pour half-and-half and coffee into a two quart saucepan, and bring to a scald over a medium-high flame whisking frequently. Line a sieve with a double layer of cheesecloth. Pour scalded mixture through lined sieve into bowl of melted chocolate, and whisk until mocha mixture is fully blended.

Whisk approximately 1 cup of mocha mixture into egg mixture to *temper*. Whisk in remaining mocha mixture, vanilla extract, and Tia Maria® without aeration. Strain through a fine sieve into a large glass measure cup, and pour evenly between prepared ramekins. Pour boiled water into roasting pan to reach three-fourths up the sides of ramekins, and place into oven. Lightly place slit sheet of foil over pan.

Bake mocha crèmes until set approximately fifty minutes. Remove from water bath to a rack, and cool completely. Wrap cooled crèmes with plastic, and refrigerate overnight.

Plating:

Gently pull crème from edge of ramekin with fingertips to release. Invert ramekin onto the center of a cold dessert plate, and tap bottom for full release. Garnish with chantilly cream, and chocolate curls.

Yield:

seven mocha crèmes

temper: to incorporate a hot liquid into an egg mixture to equalize temperature

Source Directory

Maintaining the sustainable agriculture of Vermont's legacy is what motivates these food producers and purveyors.

The impact of over cultivation of the soil with successive plantings of genetically uniform crops, the overuse of synthetic fertilizers and pesticides, and the addition of hormones and antibiotics to livestock feed spurred organic and animal husbandry farmers to commit to restoring the health of the land and the integrity of its food production.

These regional producers and purveyors of local and seasonal foods promote that commitment and help to preserve the agricultural heritage of Vermont.

Bella Bella Gourmet Foods

P.O. Box 26302

West Haven, CT 06516

Toll free: 877-513-FOOD

www.bellagourmet.com

Producer of free-roaming heirloom breeds of chickens, poussin, partridge, moulard duck, quail, pintade, rabbit, and foie gras for twenty-five years. USDA inspected.

Berry Creek Farm

P.O. Box 76

Westfield, VT 05874

802-744-2406

berrycreekfarmvt@comcast.net

Certified-organic family farm since 1992, producing strawberries, gooseberries, vegetables, and organically raised beef, pork, chicken, and more!

Bonnieview Farm

2228 South Albany Road

Craftsbury Common, VT 05827

802-755-6878

bonnieview@earthlink.net

This sheep dairy in the soul of Vermont's Northeast Kingdom, produces raw-milk cheeses and pasture-raised lambs.

Boyden Farm

44 VT. Rte. 104

Cambridge, VT 05444

802-644-6363 (retail)/ 802-644-5974 (wholesale)

www.boydenfarm.com

Naturally raised Vermont beef sold retail at the farm; sold wholesale to health food retailers.

Brattleboro Food Co-op

2 Main Street

Brattleboro, VT 05301

802-257-0236

www.brattleborofoodcoop.com

Committed to helping build and support the production of food and food-related products, locally and throughout Vermont.

Butterworks Farm

421 Trumpass Road

Westfield, VT 05874

802-744-6855

www.butterworksfarm.com

Producers of yogurt and heavy cream from organically fed Jersey cows.

Cabot Creamery

Main Street

Cabot, VT 05647

802-371-1260

www.cabotcheese.com

Farmer owned co-op manufacturing excellent award-winning dairy products since 1919.

Cavendish Game Birds

P.O. Box 27

190 Paddock Road

Springfield, VT 05156

Toll free: 800-772-0928

www.CavendishGameBirds.com

We produce the finest jumbo quail and traditional ring-necked pheasant available on the market today, and supply great chefs and restaurants across the country.

Champlain Valley Rabbitry

1725 Rte. 22A

West Haven, VT 05743

802-265-8275

info@VermontQualityRabbits.com

Top-quality New Zealand white rabbits, ensuring optimum health and size using the most advanced techniques available. Vermont State inspected.

Cherry Hill Farm

409 Highland Road

Springfield, VT 05156

802-885-5088

cherryhillfarm@vermontel.net

We grow berries and fruits, and produce our own purées and jams.

Chimayo To Go/ Cibalo Junction

HCR 65, Box 71

Ojo Sarco, NM 87521

Toll free: 800-683-9628

info@chimayotogo.com

Ojo Sarco is a small village located between Santa Fe and Taos, New Mexico, offering the highest-quality New Mexico red chile powder and products.

City Market/Onion River Co-op

82 South Winooski Ave.

Burlington, VT 05401

802-863-3659

www.citymarket.coop

Sixty cents of every dollar that goes through the cash register stays in Vermont; featuring over one thousand locally produced Vermont products.

Dakin Farm

5797 Rte. 7

Ferrisburgh, VT 05456

Toll free: 800-993-2546

www.dakinfarm.com

Mouthwatering meats smoked the old-fashioned way, over glowing corncob embers; aged Vermont cheeses; and the freshest of pure Vermont maple syrup.

Does' Leap

1703 Rte. 108 South

Fairfield, VT 05448

802-827-3046

doesleap@pshift.com

This small, certified-organic goat dairy produces high-quality goat cheeses.

Flag Hill Farm

135 Ewing Road

Vershire, VT 05079

802-685-7724

www.flaghillfarm.com

We grow eighty-seven varieties of organic apples, and produce Artisanal hard cider, Pomme de Vie, and Stair's Pear Brandy.

Grafton Village Cheese

533 Townshed Road

P.O. Box 87

Grafton, VT 05146

802-843-2221

www.graftonvillagecheese.com

We use Grafton's traditional methods of cheddar making from the late 1800s to produce excellent cheeses.

Green Mountain Blue Cheese

2183 Gore Road

Highgate Center, VT 05459-4022

802-868-4193

www.vtcheese.com

The Boucher family has produced raw-milk cheese for four hundred years.

Healthy Living

222 Dorset Street

South Burlington, VT 05403

802-863-2569

www.healthylivingmarket.com

Purveyors of fine natural, organic, and gourmet foods, where customers find local meats, fine wines, fantastic organic produce, crusty breads, cheeses from all over the world, and a staff that cares!

Highland Sugarworks

40 Pitman Road

Websterville, VT 05678

802-479-1747

info@highlandsugarwork.com

Wholesale distributor, producing pure certified-organic maple syrup delivered free to local retail outlets throughout Vermont.

Historic Craftsbury General Store

118 S. Craftsbury Road

Craftsbury, VT 05826

802-586-2893

dstember@aol.com

Purveyor of quality locally produced foods.

Hollandeer Farm

58 Stage Coach Lane

Holland, VT 05829

802-895-4115

www.hollandeerfarm.com

We produce farm-raised red deer, naturally grain-fed without hormones; selling retail, wholesale, and to restaurants.

Hunger Mountain Co-op

623 Stone Cutter Way

Montpelier, VT 05602

802-223-8000

www.hungermountain.com

We are committed to the sustainability of local food artisans, organic farmers, and meat and poultry producers. The Co-op offers a diverse selection of locally baked breads, artisan cheeses, and specialty wines and beers.

King Arthur Flour

135 Rte. 5 South

Norwich, VT 05055

802-526-1870

www.kingarthurflour.com

Founded in 1790, King Arthur Flour is the oldest flour company in the United States. We offer a full line of organic and nonorganic flours, baking products, and kitchen tools and supplies.

Lake Champlain Chocolates

750 Pine Street

Burlington, VT 05401

802-864-1808

www.lakechamplainchocolates.com

This is Vermont's all-natural chocolates.

Lazy Lady Farms

Westfield, VT 05874

www.vtcheese.com

This is a certified-organic goat dairy since 1987.

LedgeEnd Farm

1288 Munger Street

Middlebury, VT 05753

802-388-8979

ledgendeer@aldelphia.net

Vermont farm-raised fallow deer venison is naturally raised on pasture in the growing season and haylage and corn silage in winter. No growth hormones or antibiotics used. Vermont State inspected.

Maplebrook Farm

453 East Road

Bennington, VT 05201

802-440-9950

www.mountainmozzarella,com

We are Old-World cheese artisans producing fresh mozzarella without preservatives, additives, or salt.

Maple Wind Farm

1340 Carse Road

Huntington, VT 05462

802-434-7257

www.maplewindfarm.com

We are a pasture-based, diversified livestock operation producing grass-fed and finished beef and lamb, and pastured, organic poultry and pork.

Misty Knoll Farm

1685 Main Street

New Haven, VT 05472

802-453-4748

www.mistyknollfarm.com

A family-owned and -operated farm devoted to producing the finest selection of poultry and poultry products.

Pete's Greens

266 S. Craftsbury Road

Craftsbury, VT 05826

802-586-2882

We grow specialty vegetables, heirloom tomatoes, and root crops, offering the greatest diversity of vegetables for as much of the year as possible.

Ridgeway Red Deer Farm

157 Plumb Road

Whitingham, VT 05361

802-368-2556

www.ridgewayreddeerfarm.com

We offer 100 percent premium red deer venison from farm-raised deer without hormones or growth stimulants. USDA inspected, fresh-vacuum sealed and frozen.

Shelburne Farms

1611 Harbor Road

Shelburne, VT 05482

802-985-8686

www.shelburnefarms.org

We produce award-winning farmhouse cheddar cheese. Shelburne Farms is a 1,400 acre farm, national historic landmark and nonprofit environmental organization whose mission is to cultivate the conservation and stewardship of natural and agricultural resources.

Sweet Retreat Guesthouse and Sugarworks

329 Frost Road

Northfield, VT 05663

Toll free: 800-707-8427

www.SweetRetreat-Vermont.com

We produce pure Vermont Gold maple syrup in our state-of-the-art sugar house in Northfield, Vermont.

The Woodstock Water Buffalo Company

2749-01 Church Hill Road

South Woodstock, VT 05071

802-457-4540

http://bufaladivermont.com/

We are the first water buffalo dairy in the United States producing fresh buffalo milk mozzarella cheese and yogurt, and 100% water buffalo specialty meats.

Vermont Butter and Cheese Company

40 Pitman Road

Websterville, VT 05678

Toll free: 800-884-6287

www.vtbutterandcheeseco.com

Makers of fine European-style goat cheeses, cultured butter, mascarpone, crème fraîche, fromage blanc, feta, and quark cheeses.

Vermont Cranberry Company

2563 North Road

Fletcher, VT 05488

802-849-6358

vtcranco@surfglobal.net

We are Vermont's first commercial grower of cranberries, with restaurant, retail, and wholesale sales.

Vermont Herb and Salad Company

1204 Money Hole Road

Benson, VT 05743

802-537-2006

vherb@vermontel.net

We are a four-season family farm producing a wide variety of culinary herbs and greens without the use of synthetic fertilizers or pesticides; offering retail and bulk sales.

Vermont Smoke and Cure

Rte. 14

South Barre, VT 05670

802-476-4666

www.vtsmokeandcure.com

A wide selection of smoked meats, fresh sausages, and cob and Vermont maple smoked bacon, ham, and turkey.

Wood Creek Farm

560 Lake Street

Bridport, VT 05734

802-758-2909

www.woodcreekfarmbeef.com

Superior natural, 100 percent vegetarian-fed beef products grown in uncrowded pastures. Shrink wrapped and delivered fresh/frozen.

Index

A

Alfredo Sauce, 138
Appetizers
 Apricot-Glazed Shrimp Cocktail, 83
 Baby Artichoke Tart, 22
 Caramelized Sea Scallops with Clementine-Fennel
  Relish, 136
 Crab-Stuffed Chive Crêpe Pillows with Roasted
  Corn Cream, 76
 Farfalle with Cremini, Smoked Salmon, and Green
  Peppercorn, 206
 Fettuccine Alfredo, 138
 Fusilli with Pancetta, Button Mushrooms, and
  Baby Spinach, 19
 Gateau Escargot with Red Wine Gastrique, 139
 Pan-Roasted Quail with Cinnamon and French
  Lentils, 207
 Penne with Shallot, Garlic, Roma Tomato, and
  Basil, 85
 Poached Blue Mussels Vin Blanc, 17
 Pork Rillettes with Sweet Onion Marmalade and
  Cornichons, 202
 Salmon Galantine with Crème Fraîche, 14
 Spinach Lasagna, 80
 Spinach Timbales with Roasted Red Pepper Sauce,
  198
 Tourtière with Apricot-Tomato Jam, 142
Apples
 Roasted Acorn Squash and Apple Bisque, 160
 Tarte Tatin, 189
Apricot Marinade, 83
Apricot-Glazed Shrimp Cocktail, 83
Apricots
 Apricot Marinade, 83
 Apricot-Glazed Shrimp Cocktail, 83
 Apricot-Tomato Jam, 142
Apricot-Tomato Jam, 142
Artichoke
 Baby Artichoke Tart, 22
Arugula
 Baby Beet, Arugula, and Hazelnut Salad with
  Hazelnut Vinaigrette, 40
 Spring Greens, 45
Asparagus
 Asparagus, Vermont Blue, and Mâche, 43
 Chicken Roulade of Prosciutto, Asparagus, and
  Havarti, 58
Asparagus, Vermont Blue, and Mâche with Blue
 Cheese Vinaigrette, 43

Avocado
 Watercress Salad with Avocado and Shaved
  Asiago, 100

B

Baby Artichoke Tart, 22
Baby Beet, Arugula, and Hazelnut Salad with
 Hazelnut Vinaigrette, 40
Bacon
 Bacon-Ranch Dressing, 107
 Chopped Salad with Spicy Chicken and Bacon-
  Ranch Dressing, 107
Bacon-Ranch Dressing, 107
Balsamic Vinaigrette, 226
Basil
 Fresh Tomato-Basil Cream, 98
 Penne with Shallot, Garlic, Roma Tomato, and
  Basil, 85
Beans and Legumes
 Cinnamon and French Lentils, 207
 Glazed Yellow and Green Beans, 109
 Lamb Chop and Fava Bean Ragoût, 51
 White Bean and Chorizo Salad, *231*
 White Beans, *231*
Beef
 Roast Tenderloin of Beef, 242
 Teriyaki-Marinated Tri-Tip Sirloin, 114
Beets
 Baby Beet, Arugula, and Hazelnut Salad, 40
 Borscht, 39
Bell Pepper Pesto, 46
Billi Bi Soup, 162
Bing Cherry Sauce, 133
Biscuit, 61
Black Currant Dinner Rolls, 89
Black Pepper-Scented Ice Cream, 126
 Fresh Plum Tartlets with Black Pepper-Scented Ice
  Cream, 123
Blue Cheese Vinaigrette, 43
Borscht, 39
Bosc Pear with Vermont Blue and Bitter Greens with
 Balsamic Vinaigrette, 226
Bouchée, *235*
Bouchée of Lobster, Shrimp, and Broccoli Nantua,
 235
Breads
 Black Currant Dinner Rolls, 89
 Brown Bread, 210
 Cracked Wheat Rolls, 91
 Crusty Boules, 150

Focaccia, 29
Miniature Corn Muffins, 88
Olive Loaves, 215
Pain au Lait, 213
Pain Ordinare, 86
Parmesan Breadsticks, 211
Petit Pains, 25
Poppy Seed Dinner Rolls, 31
Rosemary-Raisin Baguettes, 148
Stone Ground Whole Wheat Loaves, 27
Triple-Seeded Braid, 154
Vermont Cheddar Rolls, 146
Broccoli
Bouchée of Lobster, Shrimp, and Broccoli Nantua,
235
Brook Trout
Dressed Brook Trout stuffed with Bell Pepper
Pesto, 46
Brown Bread, 210
Buffalo Mozzarella, Wild Mushroom, and Vine-
Ripened Tomato Salad, 168

C

Cabbage
Red Cabbage, 179
Caesar Dressing, 104
Caesar Salad, 104
Cakes
Biscuit, 61
Caramelized Almond and Pear Cheesecake, 247
Ganache Chocolate Mousse Cake, 119
Gateau Escargot, 139
Pistachio Sponge Cake with Mascarpone Cheese
Frosting, 61
White Chocolate Cheesecake, 186
Calamata Olive Dressing, 42
Candied Zest, 250
Caramelized Almond and Pear Cheesecake, 247
Caramelized Almonds, 172, 247
Caramelized Almond and Pear Cheesecake, 247
Red Bartlet Pear and Fontina Cheese Salad, 172
Caramelized Sea Scallops with Clementine-Fennel
Relish, 136
Carrots
Cream of Carrot-Ginger Soup, 36
Tarragon Carrots, 116
Cauliflower
Cream of Cauliflower Soup, 225
Chantilly Cream, 122
Ganache Chocolate Mousse Cake with Chantilly
Cream, 119
Hubbard Squash and Crystallized Ginger Tart with
Myers's Rum Chantilly Cream, 192

Myers's Rum Chantilly Cream, 192
Cherries
Bing Cherry Sauce, 133
Sun-Dried Cherry Sauce, 182
Venison Loin Roast with Sun-Dried Cherry Sauce,
182
White Chocolate Timbales with Bing Cherry
Sauce, 131
Chicken
Chicken Consommé, 37
Chicken Roulade of Prosciutto, Asparagus, and
Havarti, 58
Chicken Stock, 35
Chopped Salad with Spicy Chicken, 107
Coq au Vin, 174
Chicken Consommé, 37
Chicken Roulade of Prosciutto, Asparagus, and
Havarti with Morel Cream Sauce, Fiddleheads,
and Russet Potato, 58
Chicken Stock, 35
Chive Crêpe Pillows, 76
Chocolate
Chocolate Sauce, 61
Ganache Chocolate Mousse Cake, 119
Mocha Crèmes, 253
White Chocolate and Maple Mousse in Almond
Tuile, 68
White Chocolate Cheesecake, 186
White Chocolate Timbales, 131
Chocolate Sauce, 61
Chopped Salad with Spicy Chicken and Bacon-Ranch
Dressing, 107
Cinnamon and French Lentils, 207
Citrus
Candied Zest, 250
Citrus Salad, 228
Citrus Vinaigrette, 228
Clementine Marinade, 136
Clementine-Fennel Relish, 136
Key Lime Tartlets, 71
Lemon Curd, 250
Lemon Syrup, 61
Lemon Tartlets, 250
Orange-Balsamic Vinaigrette, 170
Tequilla-Lime Marinade, 111
Citrus Salad, 228
Citrus Vinaigrette, 228
Clementine Marinade, 136
Clementine-Fennel Relish, 136
Coq au Vin, 174
Corn
Corn Chowder, 93
Crab-Stuffed Chive Crêpe with Roasted Corn

Cream, 76
Miniature Corn Muffins, 88
Roasted Corn and Poblano Salsa, 111
Roasted Corn Cream, 76
Corn Chowder, 93
Crabmeat
Crab-Stuffed Chive Crêpe Pillows, 76
Crab-Stuffed Chive Crêpe Pillows with Roasted Corn
Cream, 76
Cracked Wheat Rolls, 91
Cranberries
Cranberry Vinaigrette, 166
Crispy Magret of Duckling with Fresh Cranberry
Compote, 176
Fresh Cranberry Compote, 176
Spinach Salad with Honeyed Spiked Pecans and
Gorgonzola and Cranberry Vinaigrette, 166
Cranberry Vinaigrette, 166
Cream of Carrot-Ginger Soup, 36
Cream of Cauliflower Soup, 225
Cream of Parsnip, 158
Creamy Garlic Dressing, 100
Creamy Wild Rice, 176
Crème Brûlée, 245
Crème Caramel, 184
Crème Fraîche
Roasted Acorn Squash and Apple Bisque with
Crème Fraîche, 160
Salmon Galantine with Crème Fraîche, 14
Crèmes
Crème Brûlée, 245
Crème Caramel, 184
Mocha Crèmes, 253
Crispy Leeks, 223
Crispy Magret of Duckling with Fresh Cranberry
Compote and Creamy Wild Rice, 176
Crusty Boules, 150
Currants
Black Currant Dinner Rolls, 89

D

Dessert Sauces
Bing Cherry Sauce, 133
Chocolate Sauce, 61
Fresh Raspberry Sauce, 129
Pomegranate Sauce, 188
Strawberry Sauce, 65
Desserts
Caramelized Almond and Pear Cheesecake, 247
Crème Brûlée, 245
Crème Caramel, 184
Fresh Plum Tartlets with Black Pepper-Scented Ice
Cream, 123
Ganache Chocolate Mousse Cake with Chantilly
Cream, 119
Hubbard Squash and Crystallized Ginger Tart with
Myers's Rum Chantilly Cream, 192
Key Lime Tartlets with Fruit Salsa, 71
Lemon Tartlets, 250
Mocha Crèmes, 253
Pistachio Sponge Cake with Mascarpone Cheese
Frosting and Chocolate Sauce, 61
Raspberry and Grand Marnier Soufflé Glacé with
Fresh Raspberry Sauce, 129
Strawberry Charlotte Russe with Strawberry
Sauce, 65
Tarte Tatin with Vanilla Bean Ice Cream, 189
White Chocolate and Maple Mousse in Almond
Tuile, 68
White Chocolate Cheesecake with Pomegranate
Sauce, 186
White Chocolate Timbales with Bing Cherry
Sauce, 131
Dressed Brook Trout stuffed with Bell Pepper Pesto
with Red Wine Sauce, Steamed Spinach and
Shallots, 46
Dressings
Bacon-Ranch Dressing, 107
Caesar Dressing, 104
Calamata Olive Dressing, 42
Creamy Garlic Dressing, 100
Duckling
Crispy Magret of Duckling with Fresh Cranberry
Compote, 176

E

Entrées
Bouchée of Lobster, Shrimp, and Broccoli Nantua,
235
Chicken Roulade of Prosciutto, Asparagus, and
Havarti with Morel Cream Sauce, Fiddleheads,
and Russet Potato, 58
Coq au Vin, 174
Crispy Magret of Duckling with Fresh Cranberry
Compote and Creamy Wild Rice, 176
Dressed Brook Trout stuffed with Bell Pepper
Pesto with Red Wine Sauce, Steamed Spinach
and Shallots, 46
Fillet of Sole with Fines Herbs à la Meunière with
Tarragon Carrots, 116
Lamb Chop and Fava Bean Ragoût with Whipped
Potatoes, 51
Osso Bucco, *233*
Poached Turbot with Tomato-Herb Broth, 55
Rabbit Blanquette with Straw and Hay Tagliatelle,
239

Roast Pork Loin with Rhubarb Sauce and Glazed
    Yellow and Green Beans, 109
Roast Tenderloin of Beef with Sauce au Poivre
    and Potato Dauphinoise, 242
Tequila-Lime Swordfish with Roasted Corn and
    Poblano Salsa and Parsley Red Potatoes, 111
Teriyaki-Marinated Tri-Tip Sirloin and Parmesan
    and Gruyère Whipped Potatoes, 114
Venison Loin Roast with Sun-Dried Cherry Sauce,
    182
Wiener Schnitzel with Potato Pancakes and Red
    Cabbage, 179
Escargot
    Gateau Escargot, 139
Escarole
    Salad of Escarole, Endive, and Garlic Croutons,
    230

F

Farfalle with Cremini, Smoked Salmon, and Green
    Peppercorn, 206
Fennel
    Clementine-Fennel Relish, 136
Fettuccine Alfredo, 138
Fiddleheads, 58
Fillet of Sole with Fines Herbs à la Meunière with
    Tarragon Carrots, 116
Fish
    Dressed Brook Trout stuffed with Bell Pepper
        Pesto, 46
    Fillet of Sole with Fines Herbs à la Meunière, 116
    Poached Turbot with Tomato-Herb Broth, 55
    Salmon Galantine, 14
    Tequila-Lime Swordfish, 111
Focaccia, 29
French Onion Soup, 220
Fresh Cranberry Compote, 176
Fresh Plum Tartlets with Black Pepper-Scented Ice
    Cream, 123
Fresh Raspberry Sauce, 129
Fresh Tomato-Basil Cream, 98
Fruit Salsa, 71
Fruits. *See* specific fruits
Fumet
    Blue Mussel Fumet, 17
    Fish Fumet for Billi Bi Soup, 162
    Fish Fumet for Oyster Chowder, *218*
Fusilli with Pancetta, Button Mushrooms, and Baby
    Spinach, 19

G

Ganache Chocolate Mousse Cake with Chantilly
    Cream, 119

Garlic
    Creamy Garlic Dressing, 100
    Garlic Croutons, 104
    Garlic Vinaigrette, *231*
    Penne with Shallot, Garlic, Roma Tomato, and
        Basil, 85
    Salad of Escarole, Endive, and Garlic Croutons,
        230
Garlic Croutons, 104
Garlic Vinaigrette, *231*
Gateau Escargot with Red Wine Gastrique, 139
Gazpacho, 97
Ginger
    Cream of Carrot-Ginger Soup, 36
    Hubbard Squash and Crystallized Ginger Tart, 192
Glazed Yellow and Green Beans, 109
Graham Cracker Crust, 186, 247
    Caramelized Almond and Pear Cheesecake, 247
    White Chocolate Cheesecake, 186

H

Hazelnut Pâte Sucrée, 123
Hazelnut Vinaigrette, 40
Honeyed Spiked Pecans, 166
Hubbard Squash and Crystallized Ginger Tart with
    Myers's Rum Chantilly Cream, 192

I

Ice Cream
    Black Pepper-Scented Ice Cream, 126
    Raspberry and Grand Marnier Soufflé Glacé, 129
    Vanilla Bean Ice Cream, 190

K

Key Lime Tartlets with Fruit Salsa, 71

L

Lamb
    Lamb Chop and Fava Bean Ragoût, 51
Lamb Chop and Fava Bean Ragoût with Whipped
    Potatoes, 51
Leeks
    Crispy Leeks, 223
    Potato-Leek Cream with Crispy Leeks, 223
Lemon. *See* Citrus
Lemon Curd, 250
Lemon Syrup, 61
Lemon Tartlets, 250
Lime. *See* Citrus
Lobster
    Bouchée of Lobster, Shrimp, and Broccoli Nantua,
        235

M

Mâche
Asparagus, Vermont Blue, and Mâche, 43
Spring Greens, 45
Maple Syrup
Maple-Balsamic Vinaigrette, 45
White Chocolate and Maple Mousse, 68
Maple-Balsamic Vinaigrette, 45
Marinades
Apricot Marinade, 83
Clementine Marinade, 136
Small Game Marinade, 207
Tequila-Lime Marinade, 111
Teriyaki Marinade, 114
Mascarpone Cheese Frosting, 61
Menus
Autumn, 6
Spring, 2
Summer, 4
Winter, 8
Miniature Corn Muffins, 88
Mocha Crèmes, 253
Morel Cream Sauce, 58
Mousse
Ganache Chocolate Mousse Cake, 119
White Chocolate and Maple Mousse, 68
Mushroom Cream Soup, 156
Mushrooms
Buffalo Mozzarella, Wild Mushroom, and Vine-
Ripened Tomato Salad, 168
Farfalle with Cremini, Smoked Salmon, and Green
Peppercorn, 206
Fusilli with Pancetta, Button Mushrooms, and
Baby Spinach, 19
Morel Cream Sauce, 58
Mushroom Cream Soup, 156
Mussels
Billi Bi Soup, 162
Poached Blue Mussels Vin Blanc, 17
Myers's Rum Chantilly Cream, 192

N

Nantua Sauce, *235*
Nuts
Almond Tuile, 68
Biscuit, 61
Caramelized Almonds, 172, 247
Hazelnut Pâte Sucrée, 123
Hazelnut Vinaigrette, 40
Honeyed Spiked Pecans, 166
Pistachio Sponge Cake, 61

O

Olive Loaves, 215
Olives
Calamata Olive Dressing, 42
Olive Loaves, 215
Onions
French Onion Soup, 220
Sweet Onion Marmalade, 204
Orange-Balsamic Vinaigrette, 170
Osso Bucco, *233*
Oyster Chowder, 218
Oysters
Oyster Chowder, 218

P

Pain au Lait, 213
Pain Ordinare, 86
Pancetta
Fusilli with Pancetta, Button Mushrooms, and
Baby Spinach, 19
Pan-Roasted Quail with Cinnamon and French
Lentils, 207
Parmesan and Gruyère Whipped Potatoes, 114
Parmesan Breadsticks, 211
Parsley Red Potatoes, 111
Parsnips
Cream of Parsnip, 158
Pasta
Farfalle with Cremini, Smoked Salmon, and Green
Peppercorn, 206
Fettuccine Alfredo, 138
Fusilli with Pancetta, Button Mushrooms, and
Baby Spinach, 19
Penne with Shallot, Garlic, Roma Tomato, and
Basil, 85
Spinach Lasagna, 80
Straw and Hay Tagliatelle, *239*
Pastry Doughs
Hazelnut Pâte Sucrée, 123
Pâte, 142
Pâte Brisée, 24
Pâte Sucrée, 192
Pâte, 142
Pâte Brisée, 24
Pâte Sucrée, 192
Pear Vinaigrette, 172
Pears
Bosc Pear with Vermont Blue and Bitter Greens,
226
Caramelized Almond and Pear Cheesecake, 247
Pear Vinaigrette, 172
Poached Pears, 247

Red Bartlett Pear and Fontina Cheese Salad, 172
Penne with Shallot, Garlic, Roma Tomato, and Basil, 85
Peppers
    Bell Pepper Pesto, 46
    Red Pepper Cream, 33
    Roasted Corn and Poblano Salsa, 111
    Roasted Red Pepper Sauce, 200
Pesto
    Bell Pepper Pesto, 46
Petit Pains, 25
Pistachio Sponge Cake with Mascarpone Cheese
    Frosting and Chocolate Sauce, 61
Plums
    Fresh Plum Tartlets, 123
Poached Blue Mussels Vin Blanc, 17
Poached Pears, 247
Poached Turbot with Tomato-Herb Broth, 55
Pomegranate Sauce, 188
Poppy Seed Dinner Rolls, 31
Pork
    Pork Rillettes, 202
    Roast Pork Loin with Rhubarb Sauce, 109
    Tourtière, 142
Pork Rillettes with Sweet Onion Marmalade and
    Cornichons, 202
Potato Dauphinoise, 244
Potato Pancakes, 179
Potatoes
    Parmesan and Gruyère Whipped Potatoes, 114
    Parsley Red Potatoes, 111
    Potato Dauphinoise, 244
    Potato Pancakes, 179
    Potato-Leek Cream, 223
    Sweet Potato Hash, 182
    Whipped Potatoes, 54
Potato-Leek Cream with Crispy Leeks, 223
Poultry. See Chicken, Duckling, Quail. and Turkey
Preserves
    Apricot-Tomato Jam, 142
    Fresh Cranberry Compote, 176
    Sweet Onion Marmalade, 204
Prosciutto
    Chicken Roulade of Prosciutto, Asparagus, and
        Havarti, 58

Q

Quail
    Pan-Roasted Quail with Cinnamon and French
        Lentils, 207

R

Rabbit

Rabbit Blanquette, 239
Rabbit Stock, 239
Rabbit Blanquette with Straw and Hay Tagliatelle,
    239
Rabbit Stock, 239
Raspberries
    Fresh Raspberry Sauce, 129
    Raspberry and Grand Marnier Soufflé Glacé with
        Fresh Raspberry Sauce, 129
Raspberry and Grand Marnier Soufflé Glacé with
    Fresh Raspberry Sauce, 129
Ratatouille Salad with Fresh Buffalo Mozzarella, 101
Red Bartlett Pear and Fontina Cheese Salad, 172
Red Cabbage, 179
Red Pepper Cream, 33
Red Wine Gastrique, 139
Red Wine Sauce, 46
Relish
    Clementine-Fennel Relish, 136
Remouillage, 220
Rhubarb
    Rhubarb Sauce, 109
    Roast Pork Loin with Rhubarb Sauce, 109
Rhubarb Sauce, 109
Rice
    Creamy Wild Rice, 176
    Salad of Smoked Turkey and Pecan Rice, 170
Roast Pork Loin with Rhubarb Sauce and Glazed
    Yellow and Green Beans, 109
Roast Tenderloin of Beef with Sauce au Poivre and
    Potato Dauphinoise, 242
Roasted Acorn Squash and Apple Bisque with Crème
    Fraîche, 160
Roasted Corn and Poblano Salsa, 111
Roasted Corn Cream, 76
Roasted Red Pepper Sauce, 200
Rosemary-Raisin Baguettes, 148

S

Salad of Escarole, Endive, and Garlic Croutons with
    Warm Red Wine-Mustard Vinaigrette, 230
Salad of Smoked Turkey and Pecan Rice with
    Orange-Balsamic Vinaigrette, 170
Salads
    Asparagus, Vermont Blue, and Mâche with Blue
        Cheese Vinaigrette, 43
    Baby Beet, Arugula, and Hazelnut Salad with
        Hazelnut Vinaigrette, 40
    Bosc Pear with Vermont Blue and Bitter Greens
        with Balsamic Vinaigrette, 226
    Buffalo Mozzarella, Wild Mushroom, and Vine-
        Ripened Tomato Salad, 168
    Caesar Salad, 104

Chopped Salad with Spicy Chicken and Bacon-
  Ranch Dressing, 107
Citrus Salad, 228
Ratatouille Salad with Fresh Buffalo Mozzarella,
  101
Red Bartlett Pear and Fontina Cheese Salad, 172
Salad of Escarole, Endive, and Garlic Croutons
  with Warm Red Wine-Mustard Vinaigrette,
  230
Salad of Smoked Turkey and Pecan Rice with
  Orange-Balsamic Vinaigrette, 170
Spinach and Feta Cheese Salad with Calamata
  Olive Dressing, 42
Spinach Salad with Honeyed Spiked Pecans and
  Gorgonzola and Cranberry Vinaigrette, 166
Spring Greens, 45
Watercress Salad with Avocado and Shaved
  Asiago with Creamy Garlic Dressing, 100
White Bean and Chorizo Salad, 231
Salmon
  Farfalle with Cremini, Smoked Salmon, and Green
    Peppercorn, 206
  Salmon Galantine, 14
Salsa
  Fruit Salsa, 71
  Roasted Corn and Poblano Salsa, 111
Sauce au Poivre, 242
Sauces
  Alfredo Sauce, 138
  Morel Cream Sauce, 58
  Nantua Sauce, 235
  Red Wine Sauce, 46
  Rhubarb Sauce, 109
  Roasted Corn Cream, 76
  Roasted Red Pepper Sauce, 200
  Sauce au Poivre, 242
  Sun-Dried Cherry Sauce, 182
  Teriyaki Jus, 114
  Tomato Sauce, 80
  Tomato-Herb Broth, 55
Scallops
  Caramelized Sea Scallops, 136
Seafood. See Fish; See Shellfish
Shallots
  Penne with Shallot, Garlic, Roma Tomato, and
    Basil, 85
  Steamed Spinach and Shallots, 46
Shellfish
  Apricot-Glazed Shrimp Cocktail, 83
  Billi Bi Soup, 162
  Bouchée of Lobster, Shrimp, and Broccoli Nantua,
    235
  Caramelized Sea Scallops, 136

Crab-Stuffed Chive Crêpe Pillows, 76
  Gateau Escargot, 139
  Oyster Chowder, 218
  Poached Blue Mussels Vin Blanc, 17
Shrimp
  Apricot-Glazed Shrimp Cocktail, 83
  Bouchée of Lobster, Shrimp, and Broccoli Nantua,
    235
Small Game Marinade, 207
Sole
  Fillet of Sole with Fines Herbs à la Meunière, 116
Sorrel
  Sorrel Vichyssoise, 95
Sorrel Vichyssoise, 95
Soups
  Billi Bi Soup, 162
  Borscht, 39
  Chicken Consommé, 37
  Corn Chowder, 93
  Cream of Carrot-Ginger Soup, 36
  Cream of Cauliflower Soup, 225
  Cream of Parsnip, 158
  French Onion Soup, 220
  Fresh Tomato-Basil Cream, 98
  Gazpacho, 97
  Mushroom Cream Soup, 156
  Oyster Chowder, 218
  Potato-Leek Cream with Crispy Leeks, 223
  Red Pepper Cream, 33
  Roasted Acorn Squash and Apple Bisque with
    Crème Fraîche, 160
  Sorrel Vichyssoise, 95
Source Directory. See directory of ingredient sources
Spinach
  Fusilli with Pancetta, Button Mushrooms, and
    Baby Spinach, 19
  Spinach and Feta Cheese Salad, 42
  Spinach Lasagna, 80
  Spinach Salad with Honeyed Spiked Pecans and
    Gorgonzola, 166
  Spinach Timbales, 198
  Spring Greens, 45
  Steamed Spinach and Shallots, 46
Spinach and Feta Cheese Salad with Calamata Olive
  Dressing, 42
Spinach Lasagna, 80
Spinach Salad with Honeyed Spiked Pecans and
  Gorgonzola and Cranberry Vinaigrette, 166
Spinach Timbales with Roasted Red Pepper Sauce,
  198
Spring Greens with Maple-Balsamic Vinaigrette, 45
Squash
  Hubbard Squash and Crystallized Ginger Tart, 192

Roasted Acorn Squash and Apple Bisque, 160
Steamed Spinach and Shallots, 46
Stocks
    Chicken Stock, 35
    Rabbit Stock, *239*
    Veal Stock, 49
    Vegetable Stock, 95
Stone Ground Whole Wheat Loaves, 27
Strawberries
    Strawberry Charlotte Russe, 65
    Strawberry Sauce, 65
Strawberry Charlotte Russe with Strawberry Sauce, 65
Strawberry Sauce, 65
Streusel, 123
Sugar Glaze, 245
Sun-Dried Cherry Sauce, 182
Sweet Onion Marmalade, 204
Sweet Potato Hash, 182
Swordfish
    Tequila-Lime Swordfish, 111

T

Tarragon Carrots, 116
Tarte Tatin with Vanilla Bean Ice Cream, 189
Tarts and Tartlets
    Baby Artichoke Tart, 22
    Fresh Plum Tartlets, 123
    Hubbard Squash and Crystallized Ginger Tart, 192
    Key Lime Tartlets, 71
    Lemon Tartlets, 250
    Tarte Tatin, 189
Tequila-Lime Swordfish with Roasted Corn and Poblano Salsa and Parsley Red Potatoes, 111
Tequilla-Lime Marinade, 111
Teriyaki Jus, 114
Teriyaki-Marinated Tri-Tip Sirloin and Parmesan and Gruyère Whipped Potatoes, 114
Tomato Sauce, 80
Tomatoes
    Apricot-Tomato Jam, 142
    Buffalo Mozzarella, Wild Mushroom, and Vine-Ripened Tomato Salad, 168
    Fresh Tomato-Basil Cream, 98
    Penne with Shallot, Garlic, Roma Tomato, and Basil, 85
    Poached Turbot with Tomato-Herb Broth, 55
    Tomato Sauce, 80
    Tomato-Herb Broth, 55
Tomato-Herb Broth, 55
Tourtière with Apricot-Tomato Jam, 142

Triple-Seeded Braid, 154
Turbot
    Poached Turbot with Tomato-Herb Broth, 55
Turkey
    Salad of Smoked Turkey and Pecan Rice, 170

V

Vanilla Bean Ice Cream, 190
    Tarte Tatin with Vanilla Bean Ice Cream, 190
Veal
    Osso Bucco, *233*
    Veal Stock, 49
    Wiener Schnitzel, 179
Veal Stock, 49
Vegetable Stock, 95
Vegetables. *See* specific vegetables
Venison
    Venison Loin Roast, 182
Venison Loin Roast with Sun-Dried Cherry Sauce, 182
Vermont Cheddar Rolls, 146
Vinaigrettes
    Balsamic Vinaigrette, 226
    Blue Cheese Vinaigrette, 43
    Citrus Vinaigrette, 228
    Cranberry Vinaigrette, 166
    Garlic Vinaigrette, *231*
    Hazelnut Vinaigrette, 40
    Maple-Balsamic Vinaigrette, 45
    Orange-Balsamic Vinaigrette, 170
    Pear Vinaigrette, 172
    Warm Red Wine-Mustard Vinaigrette, *230*

W

Warm Red Wine-Mustard Vinaigrette, *230*
Watercress
    Watercress Salad with Avocado and Shaved Asiago, 100
Watercress Salad with Avocado and Shaved Asiago with Creamy Garlic Dressing, 100
Whipped Potatoes, 54
White Bean and Chorizo Salad, *231*
White Beans, *231*
White Chocolate and Maple Mousse in Almond Tuile, 68
White Chocolate Cheesecake with Pomegranate Sauce, 186
White Chocolate Timbales with Bing Cherry Sauce, 131
Wiener Schnitzel with Potato Pancakes and Red Cabbage, 179

LaVergne, TN USA
14 September 2009
157835LV00001B/52/P

9 780595 431212